Songs of Ascent

A Journey of Faith

Dr. John R. Sconiers, II

Printed in the United States of America

Library of Congress Control Number: 2025910568

ISBN-13: 979-8-9862047-9-6
ISBN-13: 979-8-9862047-8-9 (e-book)

Real Moments Media
1385 Wilmington Way Suite 100
Grayson, GA 30017
www.realmomentsmedia.com

Dedicated in memory of my father, John R. Sconiers, Sr., my mom, Maybell, and my family. Thank You for your continued support and prayers in everything that I have accomplished!

The fruit of the righteous is a tree of life, And one who is wise gains souls. Proverbs 11:30

Table of Contents

Forward

Blessed are those whose strength is in you, whose hearts are set on pilgrimage. Psalm 84:5 NIV

"Pilgrims On A Journey"

The Songs of Ascent—Psalms 120 through 134—are among the most evocative and spiritually rich passages in the entire Psalter. Nestled toward the end of the Book of Psalms, these fifteen psalms have long captured the hearts of pilgrims, poets, and worshippers throughout the centuries. Traditionally sung by ancient Israelites as they journeyed "up" to Jerusalem for the great feasts of the Lord, these psalms speak powerfully into the human condition—expressing longing, lament, hope, unity, and unwavering trust in God.

This book you are about to read is a gift to all who seek a deeper understanding of Scripture, worship with intentionality, or symbolically walk the path of spiritual pilgrimage. With scholarly insight and pastoral sensitivity, the author unpacks each Song of Ascent, illuminating its historical context, theological depth, and enduring relevance for today's believer. What emerges is not just a commentary, but a companion for the journey—a guide that invites us to align our hearts with the ancient rhythms of faith, repentance, community, and praise.

As someone who has taught and preached the Psalms for decades, I can say without hesitation that this work stands apart. It bridges the academic and the devotional, offering both rigor and reverence. Whether you are a pastor preparing a sermon series, a small group leader seeking meaningful study material, or simply a follower of Christ desiring to grow closer to Him, this book will deepen your appreciation for the beauty and power of these pilgrimage songs.

I am reminded of Augustine's famous words: "Singing is for one who loves." The Songs of Ascent were never meant merely to be studied—they were written to be sung, experienced, and lived. This book helps us do just that.

Author's Preface

For the word of God is alive and active. Sharper than any double-edged sword, it penetrates even to dividing soul and spirit, joints and marrow; it judges the thoughts and attitudes of the heart. Hebrew 4:12 NIV

"Everything has a beginning"

There are moments in the life of faith when we find ourselves on the move—journeying toward something greater, seeking clarity, purpose, or even just a renewed sense of God's presence. It was during one such season in my own spiritual pilgrimage that I returned again to the Songs of Ascent (Psalms 120–134), and what I found there was more than poetic beauty or liturgical tradition. I discovered a profound map for the soul.

The fifteen psalms known as the Songs of Ascent were once sung by ancient Israelites as they made their way "up" to Jerusalem for the great annual feasts—times of worship, remembrance, and renewal. These were not merely songs for travelers; they were songs with travelers—meant to prepare hearts, unify communities, and reorient lives around the covenant promises of God. And yet, despite their rich theological texture and enduring spiritual relevance, these psalms often remain overlooked or underappreciated in contemporary Christian life.

This book was born out of a conviction: that the Songs of Ascent have much to say to modern believers who are navigating their own journeys of faith. Whether you are walking through seasons of hardship, seeking deeper intimacy with God, or simply longing for a truer vision of worship and community, these psalms offer wisdom that transcends time and culture.

Over the years of teaching, preaching, and personally meditating on these texts, I began to see patterns—themes of repentance, trust, unity, humility,

3

joy, and divine provision—that form a kind of spiritual itinerary. This book is not merely a commentary, though it draws deeply from historical, literary, and theological scholarship. It is also a companion—a guide to help readers enter into the world of these psalms and allow them to speak afresh into our modern context.

My hope is that this work will serve pastors preparing sermons, small groups engaging Scripture together, and individuals seeking encouragement on their walk with Christ. Each chapter explores one psalm in depth, offering historical background, literary insight, theological reflection, and practical application. Taken together, the Songs of Ascent reveal a beautiful rhythm of ascent—not just geographically toward Jerusalem, but spiritually toward the heart of God.

As you read, may your steps be directed upward, your heart be stirred toward worship, and your soul be refreshed by the enduring truth of God's Word.

How To Use This Book

The Songs of Ascent: Before you Begin.

"May The Lord Use You Mightily"

Thank you for picking up this book. My prayer is that it will serve not only as a guide to the biblical texts known as the Songs of Ascent—Psalms 120 through 134—but also as a spiritual companion on your journey toward deeper intimacy with God. These psalms were once sung by pilgrims making their way to Jerusalem, ascending toward the presence of the Lord in worship and joy. Today, they remain powerful expressions of faith, repentance, hope, and unity—offering every believer a sacred rhythm for personal devotion, corporate preaching, and small group study.

As a Devotional Guide:

Each chapter of this book is designed to be read slowly, reflectively, and prayerfully. You may choose to read one chapter per day, allowing each psalm to shape a week of personal reflection. Begin by reading the psalm itself aloud, then turn to the corresponding chapter for context, insight, and application. Consider journaling your thoughts or memorizing key verses as you walk through these songs. Whether you're beginning your day with the Lord or winding down in quiet reflection, these pages are meant to draw your heart upward into His presence.

For Preaching and Sermon Preparation:

Pastors and teachers will find in this book a rich resource for crafting biblically grounded, Christ-centered messages. Each chapter includes historical background, literary structure, theological themes, and pastoral applications that can form the foundation of a sermon. Because the Songs of Ascent follow a natural progression—beginning with cries from distress and moving toward praise, unity, and divine blessing—they offer an ideal framework for a multi-week sermon series. You might consider organizing your series around key themes such as pilgrimage, trust, community, humility, joy, and divine provision. The insights offered here will help you preach with both depth and relevance, connecting ancient truths with modern hearts.

For Small Group and Congregational Study:

This book also serves as an excellent tool for small group leaders and Bible study facilitators. Each chapter will leave you with thought-provoking discussions and encourage personal reflection and group interaction. This book is designed to invite participants into deeper engagement with Scripture, prompting honest conversations about struggle, faith, and God's faithfulness. You may choose to meet weekly or biweekly, pairing each session with prayer, shared testimony, and even music or creative expression that reflects the theme of ascent. By walking through these psalms together, your group will not only grow in knowledge but also in unity and spiritual depth. In all these ways—whether alone before the Lord, behind a pulpit, or gathered with others—you will find that the Songs of Ascent are more than poetic relics of the past. They are living, breathing invitations to draw near to God. Remember: the goal is not simply to teach about the Songs of Ascent, but to dwell on and enter them—to allow their ancient melodies to awaken fresh worship and devotion in your heart and the hearts of those you lead. May this book be more than a study guide; may it become a map for your journey upward, drawing you and your community ever closer to the heart of God. My hope is that this book becomes a trusted companion for your journey, guiding you ever upward in faith, worship, and love.

With gratitude, encouragement and anticipation for what God will do through His leading and your faithful leadership.

Introduction

Dear Reader,

Before we begin our ascent together, I want to invite you—personally and sincerely—into a journey that has been both scholarly and deeply spiritual for me. This book is not just an academic exploration of Psalms 120–134, often called the Songs of Ascent . It is a pilgrimage guide—a companion for those who long to draw closer to God through His Word.

Imagine, if you will, standing at the edge of a winding path that leads upward through rugged terrain toward a sacred destination. The sun is rising behind you, casting long shadows ahead. You are not the first to walk this road. Generations before us have made their way along this same route, singing songs of hope, lament, trust, and praise as they climbed. These fifteen psalms were their soundtrack—and they can be yours too.

In ancient times, faithful Israelites would make pilgrimages to Jerusalem three times a year—to celebrate Passover, Pentecost, and Tabernacles. As they traveled, often from distant villages and across harsh landscapes, they sang these Songs of Ascent. Each step brought them nearer to the house of the Lord, and each song prepared their hearts for worship. But these psalms were never meant only for ancient pilgrims. They speak powerfully into our modern journeys—our struggles with doubt, our longing for peace, our desire for deeper fellowship with God and one another. They remind us that faith is not static; it moves. It climbs. It seeks. And in seeking, it finds the One who meets us on the road.

As we explore each psalm, I'll walk with you through its historical setting, literary structure, and theological riches. But more than that, I want to help you live these psalms. To pray them. To sing them. To let them shape your heart and transform your walk with the Lord.

So, friend, before we take our first step, pause for a moment. Take a deep breath. Quiet your heart. Whether you come with joy or weariness, questions or quiet confidence, know this: you are not walking alone. God is waiting to meet you in these ancient words. And I am honored to be your guide. Let us begin our ascent.

In Grace and Truth,
Dr. John R. Sconiers II

Chapter 1

The Songs of Ascent: A guide to God

We are about to embark on a journey together. As we begin this journey through a remarkable collection of psalms—Psalms 120 to 134, known as the "Songs of Ascents" or "songs for going up." These ancient poems have resonated for centuries, offering both spiritual guidance and a window into the hopes and struggles of the Israelites. Before we explore each psalm individually, let's consider their history, purpose, and enduring relevance.

What is the secret to navigating life's turbulent journey with hope and confidence? Can we really find solace amid chaos and uncertainty? The Songs of Ascents hold answers that are as relevant now as they were thousands of years ago. These psalms are not just relics of a distant faith; they speak directly to anyone who has ever felt weary from life's journey, who has longed for refuge, or yearned for a deeper sense of purpose.

Historically, these psalms accompanied the Israelites during their pilgrimages to Jerusalem—the city set on a hill, the place God chose for His name to dwell (Exodus 34:24). Three times a year, during the major festivals—Passover, Pentecost, and Tabernacles—Israelite men were required to ascend to the temple in Jerusalem, as instructed in the Torah (Exodus 34:23-24). The ascent was both literal and symbolic: a climb up the hills to worship and a spiritual elevation toward God.

The Songs of Ascents reflect this pilgrimage, capturing the prayers, hopes, and struggles of the Israelites as they journeyed. Whether sung by pilgrims on the road, chanted by Levites ascending the steps of the temple, or recited during the period of Ezra and Nehemiah as exiles returned to a rebuilt Jerusalem, these psalms became woven into the fabric of Israel's identity.

But the relevance of these songs isn't confined to ancient Israel. The journey they describe—full of challenges, longing, and eventual arrival—mirrors the spiritual pilgrimage of believers today. John Bunyan's "The Pilgrim's Progress" famously illustrates that the Christian life is a journey from redemption toward the promised land, with its own trials and ultimate restoration. The idea of pilgrimage, then, is not just about physical travel but about the ongoing quest for God's presence and purpose.

Scholars have observed that these fifteen psalms are thoughtfully arranged, almost like a tapestry or a series of steps, each one representing a phase of the journey. Alec Motyer suggests viewing them in groups of three: a problem or distress, a cry to the Lord, and a resolution or arrival. For instance, Psalm 120 voices grief and frustration among adversaries; Psalm 121 pleads for help and assurance of God's protection; and Psalm 122 celebrates arrival and peace in Jerusalem. This pattern of struggle, supplication, and resolution runs through the entire collection.

The themes of the Songs of Ascents are rich and varied. Repentance is a recurring note, urging a return to God and acceptance of His mercy. There is a deep longing for God's presence, symbolized by the journey to Jerusalem but also by the inward desire for closeness with the divine. These psalms speak of God's dynamic involvement in the lives of His people—offering forgiveness, protection, and steadfast love. Psalm 121, for instance, assures us that "The Lord will watch over your life and keep you from all harm," a promise that brings comfort to anyone facing uncertainty.

Another powerful theme is the sovereignty of God—His absolute authority and care, even when circumstances seem chaotic or overwhelming. The psalms remind us that, despite our struggles, there is a higher power guiding our steps, just as He did for the ancient travelers. This sense of trust and dependence on God's protection is timeless, offering encouragement for our own journeys, whatever form they may take.

The Songs of Ascents also celebrate restoration and renewal, particularly after seasons of hardship or exile. Psalm 126, for example, rejoices in the return from captivity, painting a picture of joyous homecoming and gratitude for God's intervention. These moments of deliverance and hope resonate with anyone who has experienced a period of loss followed by restoration, whether spiritual, emotional, or physical.

The arrangement of these psalms is deliberate, with contributions from authors like David and Solomon, and their structure suggests a narrative of spiritual progress—a movement from distress and yearning to joy and fulfillment in God's presence. Each psalm can be seen as a step along the way, covering everything from the pain of exile to the delight of arrival, from the anxiety of the journey to the peace of worship.

Even now, the Songs of Ascents offer a model for approaching God: with expectation, confidence, and humility. They invite both individual reflection and communal worship, encouraging us to bring our burdens, our gratitude, and our hopes before God. Including these psalms in our own spiritual practices can bridge the gap between ancient faith and present-day devotion, connecting us to the experiences and prayers of those who went before us. As we embark on this study, let these old songs be our guide. Picture the Israelites climbing the hills, their voices rising in song, their hearts lifting as they draw closer to God. Imagine the joy of arrival, the relief of burdens lifted, and the assurance of God's unfailing love. Visualize your spiritual path as one that is paved with obstacles, opportunities, and moments of divine guidance. Allow the Psalms of Ascent to accompany you on your spiritual journey, reminding you of God's steadfast presence and the hope that awaits at every step.

In the chapters ahead, we'll look closely at each psalm—beginning with Psalm 120—exploring how these ancient songs intersect with our own lives and how they can encourage us on our journey of faith. The Psalms of Ascent offer a powerful parallel for this journey, emphasizing the value of group worship, reliance on God, and finding joy in the midst of adversity. These teachings have a profound impact on how we live our lives today, changing the way we think about faith and giving us a fresh sense of purpose and hope. Whether you're seeking hope, longing for direction, or simply wanting to grow closer to God, may these psalms offer wisdom, comfort, and inspiration for the road ahead.

Chapter 2

Psalm 120: Prayer For Rescue From The Treacherous.

1 I cried to the Lord in my trouble,
And He answered me.
2 Rescue my soul, Lord, from lying lips,
From a deceitful tongue.
3 What will He give to you, and what more will He do to you,
You deceitful tongue?
4 Sharp arrows of the warrior,
With the burning coals of the broom tree!
5 Woe to me, for I reside in Meshech,
For I have settled among the tents of Kedar!
6 Too long has my soul had its dwelling
With those who hate peace.
7 I am for peace, but when I speak,
They are for war.

Psalm 120 stands as the first of the Songs of Ascent, and it's not just a historical note—it's a song that still echoes in the hearts of anyone who's ever felt caught in a world of chaos, longing for peace. This psalm is raw and honest, the cry of someone who's had enough of lies, conflict, and misunderstanding. It's a prayer in times of trouble—a blueprint for how to move through distress with faith rather than fury.

Before diving into the lessons, let's look at how this psalm is built. Psalm 120 starts with a direct prayer: "In my distress, I called to the Lord, and

He answered me." The structure is simple but profound: first a desperate cry, then a plea for deliverance from deceit, followed by lament over living among people who hate peace. The language is vivid. The psalmist talks about Meshech and Kedar—places associated with strife and hostility. The message is clear: even when surrounded by trouble, the psalmist seeks God, not revenge. He longs for shalom, which means more than just the absence of conflict—it's wholeness, right relationships, and God's presence in the middle of the mess.

When the psalmist is surrounded by enemies and trouble, he doesn't fake composure or hide his pain. He brings his distress straight to God. "In my distress, I cried unto the Lord, and he heard me." There's no sugarcoating here. This is a model for us: prayer isn't about pretending everything's fine or waiting until we have it all together. God welcomes our raw, unfiltered cries. David's example is a reminder that crying out isn't weakness—it's trust. Sometimes, the bravest thing you can do is admit you can't handle it alone.

David's confidence shines through: God not only hears, but answers. "He heard me." In a world that can feel indifferent, this is a radical truth. Our prayers don't just float into the void. God is present, attentive, and listening even to the smallest, most desperate cries. David didn't need the perfect words—he just needed honesty. Scripture is full of reminders that God's ear is bent toward His children, catching every word, every sigh, even the prayers we can't quite speak. This confidence is transformative: we don't have to carry our burdens alone.

Lies are a recurring theme in Psalm 120: "Deliver my soul, O Lord, from lying lips, and from a deceitful tongue." The psalmist knows firsthand the destruction that comes from deceit. Lies can warp our relationships, twist our perceptions, and even shake our view of ourselves and God. They're subtle, spreading quickly and cutting deep. But the psalmist doesn't seek to outwit his enemies—he asks God for deliverance. This is crucial: when we're stuck in webs of deception, whether from others or from the lies we believe about ourselves, God is the one who can set us free. Proverbs 12:22 says, "The Lord detests lying lips, but he delights in people who are trustworthy." Deliverance isn't about winning arguments; it's about standing in God's truth. Words matter. "The tongue has the power of life and death" (Proverbs

18:21). The psalmist's plea shows how words can cut, distort, and destroy. Lies don't just alter circumstances—they can unravel trust, damage communities, and erode peace. The Bible is clear: God takes lying seriously because it sows discord and tears at the fabric that holds us together. In our own lives, the consequences of deceit may be quiet but deep, corroding our integrity and relationships. The antidote is to live in truth—choosing honesty over comfort, refusing to spin facts or hide behind silence when words are needed. Ephesians 4:25 urges us to "put off falsehood and speak truthfully." Truth builds; lies destroy.

The psalmist's lament, "I am for peace: but when I speak, they are for war," is painfully relatable. Sometimes, seeking peace feels like swimming against a tide of hostility. Shalom is more than just quiet—it's the active presence of God, restoring relationships and bringing justice. The pursuit of peace is intentional, not passive. Romans 12:18 puts it simply: "If it is possible, as far as it depends on you, live at peace with everyone." We can't control others, only our own hearts and responses. Pursuing peace means training ourselves to answer conflict with love rather than anger, reflecting God's presence instead of echoing the chaos around us.

Jesus affirmed this calling: "Blessed are the peacemakers, for they shall be called children of God" (Matthew 5:9). Peace isn't about avoiding conflict, but carrying God's presence into the most difficult places. Even when misunderstood or outnumbered, our comfort lies in knowing God honors these efforts. Peace isn't the absence of trouble; it's the assurance of God with us, making us instruments of His reconciliation one gentle response at a time.

Here's the paradox woven through Psalm 120: those who pursue peace often find themselves in conflict. Jesus Himself said, "I did not come to bring peace but a sword" (Matthew 10:34). True peace—rooted in God's righteousness—brings resistance. Living as a peacemaker in a broken world takes courage. Paul wrote, "Everyone who wants to live a godly life in Christ Jesus will be persecuted" (2 Timothy 3:12). Standing for righteousness and truth often puts us at odds with the world, but that's not a reason to shrink back. Jesus warned His followers that the world would hate them, just as it hated Him (John 15:18). Yet, persecution for the sake of peace is a blessing:

"Blessed are those who are persecuted because of righteousness, for theirs is the kingdom of heaven" (Matthew 5:10). Whenever opposition comes, we're standing with Christ Himself.

Psalm 120 doesn't shy away from the reality of darkness—seasons when distress seems overwhelming and hope is hard to find. Yet, in these times, God's light shines brightest. The psalmist's cry is proof that God's presence is never far, even when it feels like we're walking through the valley of the shadow of death. "God is our refuge and strength, always ready to help in times of trouble" (Psalm 46:1). We're not strong because we never stumble, but because God's light guides us, comforts us, and reminds us we're not alone. Jesus said, "I am the light of the world. Whoever follows me will never walk in darkness, but will have the light of life" (John 8:12). Fixing our eyes on His promises, we find the courage to take the next step, trusting that His word is a lamp for our feet, even when the path is unclear.

As we continue through the Songs of Ascent, the journey doesn't get easier, but it does get clearer: God is our helper, our deliverer, our source of peace and truth. Psalm 120 urges us to be peacemakers in a world of warriors—to carry God's kingdom wherever we go, changing the atmosphere with each kind word and gentle response. In moments of tension, when a prayer is all we have, we can trust that God is with us, cheering us on, lighting our way. Psalm 120 is more than a historical prayer—it's a call for today. Cry out in distress, trust that God hears, seek deliverance from deception, guard your words, pursue peace, expect resistance, and cling to God's light in the darkness. In all circumstances, let these lessons guide your prayer in times of trouble, knowing that God's presence is your anchor, your comfort, and your peace.

Even as we pursue peace, often our efforts are met with antagonism, and yet the peace of God is continually with the upright. As this psalm moves through the destructive nature of the antagonist, to the consistent confidence provided in the presence of God, he calls us to integrity, trust, and confidence in the promises of God. Though trials and persecution come, we are called unto His peace - a peace that steadies, renews, and then shines forth through us.

May we be comforted in knowing God's peace walks beside us through every season, through every test of character, into final rest in His eternal peace and the understanding that a simple prayer "O Lord Help Me!" is more than enough!

Chapter 3

Psalm 121: The Lord, The Keeper of Israel.

1I will raise my eyes to the mountains;
From where will my help come?
2 My help comes from the Lord,
Who made heaven and earth.
3 He will not allow your foot to slip;
He who watches over you will not slumber.
4 Behold, He who watches over Israel
Will neither slumber nor sleep.
5 The Lord is your [a]protector;
The Lord is your shade on your right hand.
6 The sun will not [b]beat down on you by day,
Nor the moon by night.
7 The Lord will [c]protect you from all evil;
He will keep your soul.
8 The Lord will [d]guard your going out and your coming in
From this time and forever.

As we reflect together on Psalm 121, we must understand it is one of the most cherished of the Songs of Ascents. This ancient song, sung by travelers ascending toward Jerusalem, has echoed through the centuries as both a historic prayer and a present source of strength. Whether read individually or as a community, Psalm 121 has become known as "God's Protection Prayer," offering comfort and anchoring our faith in every season of life.

The psalm opens with a scene many of us know all too well: standing at the foot of life's mountains, wondering where our help will come from. "I lift up my eyes to the hills. Where does my help come from? My help comes from the Lord, who made heaven and earth." These words are personal, intimate—a cry from an individual heart. Yet as the psalm unfolds, it shifts from "I" and "my" to "you" and "your," drawing the whole community of pilgrims into its embrace. This movement from private longing to shared faith reminds us that our walk with God is both personal and collective, that faith is nurtured in solitude and sustained in fellowship.

Much has been made of those hills the psalmist gazes at. Some see them as symbols of anxiety and danger, a reminder of the brigands and hardships that threatened ancient travelers. Others view them as a sign of hope, the hills of Zion promising safety and the presence of God. Either way, the act of lifting one's eyes is an act of faith—a refusal to be defined by fear, and a turning toward the One who made the mountains and everything beyond them.

The psalm's assurance is not that life will be free from trouble, but that in all circumstances—amid the heat of day or the shadows of night—God's watchful care does not waver. "He who keeps you will not slumber; behold, He who keeps Israel will neither slumber nor sleep." This is a declaration that God is not distant observer but an ever-present Guardian. Unlike human helpers, who may falter or fail, our Protector is always vigilant, never distracted or weary. The psalmist draws out this truth with intimate imagery: the Lord as our shade, our shelter from sun and moon, a shield against life's extremes.

This theme of keeping—of God as our Keeper—weaves through every verse. The Hebrew word for "keep", shamar (□□□□□□), appears repeatedly, stressing the totality of God's protection. "The Lord will keep you from all harm—He will watch over your life; the Lord will watch over your coming and going both now and forevermore." This is not a promise of a trouble-free existence; rather, it is an assurance that, no matter what valleys or peaks we traverse, God's care is comprehensive and enduring. The psalmist's confidence is not rooted in circumstance but in the character of God: Creator of heaven and earth, Redeemer, and unfailing Companion.

Life, as we know, is a journey full of both predictable routines and unexpected turns. For the ancient Israelites, the ascent to Jerusalem was physically demanding and fraught with risks—rough mountains, changing climates, and threats from robbers. The psalm acknowledges these dangers, yet leads us to a deeper truth: our help does not ultimately come from our own strength or resources, nor from the transient security of people or possessions. "If your help does not come from God, you're making a costly mistake," the commentary reminds us. Human helpers, though well-intentioned, are limited. But the Lord's ability to help is limitless, rooted in His eternal nature. The psalm's promise is holistic. God's vigilance encompasses every aspect of our being—body, mind, and spirit. When we are active or at rest, awake or asleep, His protection is total. "The sun shall not strike you by day, nor the moon by night," the psalmist proclaims. This is more than poetry; it is the testimony of a God who cares for every detail, who shields us in ways seen and unseen.

It's important to recognize that God's protection does not mean we will never face hardship. Scripture is clear—life brings battles, as Ephesians reminds us, and the enemy is real. Yet the message of Psalm 121 is that, even in adversity, nothing can afflict us outside God's permission. His "keeping" is not passive but active; not distant but deeply engaged. He leads, disciplines, and strengthens us, building our resilience and teaching us to trust.

This psalm has long been a refuge for those needing courage in hard times. Its final verses ring out a timeless promise: "from this time forth and even forevermore." God's protection is not bound by the limits of time or the shifts of circumstance. Morning to evening, birth to old age, calm or storm— He is our Keeper. His love is timeless and boundless, a covering that endures through every season of life.

For all who feel weary, uncertain, or alone, Psalm 121 stands as an invitation: look up, lift your eyes, and see the God who walks beside you. You are neither abandoned nor overlooked. Whether your journey is physical, emotional, or spiritual, you travel with a Guide and Guard whose promise never fails.

As we conclude this reflection, let us take to heart the psalmist's assurance. God's watchfulness is immediate and eternal; His protection is as near as our next breath. Our strength does not lie in our own abilities but in His unbreakable commitment. Let these words shape your days: you are loved, looked after, and escorted through whatever life brings.

Let us be intentional about trusting God's steady hand. There will be valleys and peaks, but we never walk them alone. Lean fully into God who is constantly watching, loving, and protecting you. May your heart find comfort in His care and rise boldly each morning, for He goes before you—now and always.

Chapter 4

Psalm 122: Prayer For The Peace Of Jerusalem.

1I was glad when they said to me,
"Let's go to the house of the Lord."
2 Our feet are standing
Within your gates, Jerusalem,
3 Jerusalem, that has been built
As a city that is firmly joined together;
4 To which the tribes go up, the tribes of [a]the Lord—
[b]An ordinance for Israel—
To give thanks to the name of the Lord.
5 For thrones were set there for judgment,
The thrones of the house of David.
6 Pray for the peace of Jerusalem:
"May they prosper who love you.
7 May peace be within your walls,
And prosperity within your palaces."
8 For the sake of my brothers and my friends,
I will now say, "May peace be within you."
9 For the sake of the house of the Lord our God,
I will seek your good.

Psalm 122, a song that celebrates Jerusalem, the city at the heart of Israel's worship and is a psalm of arrival. It describes the joy of reaching Jerusalem, the thrill of standing at the gates of God's house, and the deep sense of belonging that comes with joining others in worship. The psalm unfolds in three movements: first, the joy of entering Jerusalem (verses 1-2); then, praise for the city's strength, its unity, and role as a gathering place (verses 3-5); and finally, a call to pray for the peace and well-being of Jerusalem (verses 6-9).

Jerusalem, as described in the psalm, is "knit together as a single unit" (Psalm 122:3). Its unity and security are a reflection of what God desires for His people. The city is not just a place, but a symbol—a place where God dwells, where justice is upheld, and where the community finds refuge and identity. The pilgrimage to Jerusalem is more than a physical journey; it's a movement from separation to presence, from longing to fulfillment. In the light of the gospel, this celebration of Jerusalem points us beyond its physical walls. Jesus Christ is the fulfillment of all that Jerusalem represents—He is our true home, our security, our peace. Our pilgrimage is to God in Jesus, who gathers us as living stones into a spiritual house.

But what does it mean to worship in this new Jerusalem, in the kingdom Jesus inaugurates? Real worship is not compartmentalized to a particular place or time. As Paul writes in Romans 12:1, it means presenting our bodies as living sacrifices, holy and pleasing to God. Worship happens in the everyday—at work, in relationships, in moments of solitude or service. It's a lifestyle, an alignment of everything we do with the will of God.

The unity of Jerusalem in Psalm 122 is a model for what worship is meant to be: cohesive, not fragmented. True worship brings every part of our lives into harmony as an offering to God. It's not simply about Sunday gatherings or rituals, but about a heart surrendered to God, compelled by the witness of His goodness and grace. Mary of Bethany, who anointed Jesus' feet with perfume and dried them with her hair (John 12:3), embodied this kind of worship—extravagant, personal, and authentic. Her act was not for show, but a response to who Jesus is. In contrast, Jesus criticized the Pharisees for their outward religiosity that lacked true devotion (Matthew 15:8-9). Worship without authenticity is empty.

Throughout history, lives like Mother Teresa's have shown us that worship can be silent, humble acts of love—serving the poor, comforting the suffering. Eric Liddell, the Olympic runner who refused to run on Sunday, reminds us that worship means honoring God above all else, even at personal cost. These stories challenge us to reflect on our own testimony: Does our worship flow from a surrendered, grateful, and obedient heart? Does it shape every corner of our lives?

In Psalm 122, the tribes of Israel go up together to worship, each tribe distinct yet united in purpose. This diversity within unity is a profound principle that God delights in. The Church today is the spiritual fulfillment of these tribes—one body, many members, called from every nation, language, and background. Our differences are not obstacles but gifts, adding richness to our collective praise. As Paul writes in Galatians 3:28, "There is neither Jew nor Gentile, neither slave nor free, nor is there male and female, for you are all one in Christ Jesus." God's design is not uniformity, but harmony—a unity that celebrates variety.

Yet, the Church is often weakened by division and denominationalism, losing sight of our central purpose to glorify Christ. Jesus prayed for our unity (John 17:23), knowing that our oneness would testify to the world of God's love. There will be no denominations in heaven, only a multitude of worshipers before God's throne. Shouldn't we seek that same unity here and now? Breaking down barriers takes humility and love, focusing on what binds us together: faith in Christ and the mission to advance His kingdom. Like a choir that finds its power in harmony, not in everyone singing the same note, the Church's strength lies in its united diversity. When we come together, bringing our unique gifts and perspectives, we reflect God's creativity and fulfill our purpose—to glorify Christ and serve Him and His will.

The throne, the testimony, and the tribe—these are central images in Psalm 122, and they reveal something essential about God's vision for His people. Worship is not confined to songs or ceremonies; it's a surrendered, Spirit-filled life that brings God pleasure. The testimony is not just a story, but a living witness of God's faithfulness in us. The tribe is not just a group, but a body united in love, purpose, and praise.

As we journey together, let's tear down the walls that divide, and let our lives become acts of worship that point to the glory of God. Let's use our gifts for His purpose, strengthen the bonds of the Church, and advance His kingdom on earth. God is calling us to rise in unity and truth, to live as testimonies of His love and power. Will you answer the call? Together, let's reflect heaven on earth, as one people gathered in the name of Jesus.

Chapter 5

Psalm 123: Prayer for The Lord's Help.

1 To You I have raised my eyes,
You who are enthroned in the heavens!
2 Behold, as the eyes of servants look to the hand of their master,
As the eyes of a female servant to the hand of her mistress,
So our eyes look to the Lord our God,
Until He is gracious to us.
3 Be gracious to us, Lord, be gracious to us,
For we have had much more than enough of contempt.
4 Our soul has had much more than enough
Of the scoffing of those who are at ease,
And with the contempt of the proud.

Psalm 123 stands out as a powerful example of what it means to cry out for mercy amid adversity. It is one of the Songs of Ascents, sung by pilgrims on their journey to Jerusalem, and captures the spiritual posture required when facing contempt, scorn, and overwhelming need. Through its verses—and through the stories and teachings echoed in the rest of Scripture—we see that prayers for mercy are not just desperate pleas, but profound acts of faith, humility, and dependence on God alone.

Psalm 123, like Psalm 120, addresses the challenges pilgrims faced—difficulties that are not so different from what believers encounter today. These Songs of Ascents often move in cycles: the first song in each set describes hardship, the second expresses trust, and the third brings resolution or safety. In Psalm 123, the crisis is clear: the pilgrim is worn down by contempt and scorn from the proud and the complacent (v.4). This is the experience of living among people who do not share faith in the Lord—where open devotion is not met with understanding, but with disregard or ridicule.

This pattern repeats throughout Scripture. Imagine being trapped in a life of constant need—helpless, desperate, overshadowed by forces you can't control. Blind Bartimaeus, for example, sat by the roadside, ignored by the crowd, until his piercing cry, "Son of David, have mercy on me!" (Mark 10:47), stopped Jesus in His tracks. Similarly, ten lepers at the margins of society cried out, "Jesus, Master, have pity on us!" (Luke 17:13). Their lives were transformed not by penance, but by God's mercy. These stories show us: mercy is not reserved for those seeking forgiveness alone, but is the divine bridge between human frailty and God's sufficiency.

The psalmist's first move is crucial: "I lift up my eyes to you, to you who sit enthroned in heaven." (Psalm 123:1). This is not a glance for help among many options—it is a focused, total dependence. God is not a contingency plan. He alone is the source of mercy; He must be approached as the only option.

This is a profound revelation about how to pray for mercy. We often treat God as a last resort, but Psalm 123 models something different. In desperate need, the psalmist looks up—not to the mountains, nor to idols or human solutions, but to the One enthroned in heaven. "You shall have no other gods before me," says the Lord (Exodus 20:3). When we pray for mercy, we are called to come to Him as Lord, with no backup plan, no divided allegiance.

Even in human courts, mercy can be extended, but it is always limited. Some crimes are considered beyond mercy. With God, there is no such limitation. Nineveh was a city so wicked that God had planned its destruction (Jonah 3:4). Yet, when the people repented and cried out for mercy, God forgave them. His mercy overrode judgment. Similarly, the Apostle Paul, once the chief persecutor of Christians, was transformed by God's mercy into one of history's greatest apostles (Acts 8:1-3).

God's mercy is unique: it not only reduces the punishment, but it can erase guilt completely. "Though your sins are like scarlet, they shall be as white as snow" (Isaiah 1:18). This is the mercy available to all who, like the psalmist, lift their eyes to the throne of grace.

Mercy is not automatic. Psalm 123—and the stories surrounding it—make clear that the posture of our hearts matters deeply. God is "rich in mercy" (Ephesians 2:4), but He says, "I will have mercy on whom I will have mercy" (Exodus 33:19). What moves God to show mercy?

First, humility is essential. Jonah ran from his mission to Nineveh because he knew God's mercy was so vast that even a city as wicked as Nineveh could be spared if they repented. Jonah's struggle reflects a simple truth: God's mercy is available to the humble, to those who admit their need and turn from self-righteousness. As God declares to Moses on Sinai, "The Lord, the Lord, the compassionate and gracious God, slow to anger, abounding in love and faithfulness" (Exodus 34:6).

Second, faith and obedience open the door to mercy. Psalm 123:2 paints the picture of servants watching their master, waiting for the slightest signal—a posture of total attention and readiness. Praying for mercy is not passive; it is an active, trusting dependence. Blind Bartimaeus had to get up, throw off his cloak, and move toward Jesus before being healed. The ten lepers, when told to show themselves to the priests, obeyed a command that made little sense until they acted in faith—and were healed as they went (Luke 17:11-19).

Third, brokenness matters. Psalm 51:17 reminds us, "The sacrifices of God are a broken spirit; a broken and contrite heart, O God, you will not despise." The tax collector in Jesus' parable stood far off, beat his chest, and prayed, "God, have mercy on me, a sinner" (Luke 18:13-14). He, not the self-righteous Pharisee, went home justified. Mercy flows to those who come with nothing but a desperate awareness of their need.

Dependency on God for mercy is not a one-time event. Psalm 123 describes a daily, persistent gaze. "As the eyes of servants look to the hand of their master...so our eyes look to the Lord our God, till he shows us his mercy" (v.2). This is not a casual glance but a steady, unwavering focus.

Persistence is key. Jesus told the parable of the persistent widow (Luke 18:1-8) to show that relentless prayers for mercy move the heart of God. The psalmist did not look to God once and move on; he waited, steadfast, until mercy came. God's mercy is a perpetual flow to those who remain dependent and persistent.

God knows our troubles before we speak, but He still calls us to bring them before Him. "Do not be anxious about anything, but in every situation, by prayer and petition, with thanksgiving, present your requests to God" (Philippians 4:6). In Psalm 123:3-4, the psalmist pours out his heart: "We have had more than enough of contempt. Our soul has had more than enough of the scorn of those who are at ease, of the contempt of the proud." This honest engagement is part of the process—mercy is not accessed by silent suffering, but by bold, sincere prayer.

Understanding God as the ultimate source of mercy changes everything about how we pray. We come with reverence, with hearts fully aware that He alone can transform our lives. Prayers for mercy are not empty words—they spring from a heart posture that acknowledges God as the compassionate Savior.

Let this truth settle deep: God's mercy can wipe away the worst of sins, heal the deepest wounds, restore after the most costly mistakes, and rewrite the most broken stories. It's available in every area of your life, but it starts with one thing: recognizing God as the source, and coming to Him with total dependence.

Psalm 123 calls us to a "gazeful" life—one fixed on God alone. Total dependence means faith, obedience, brokenness, and perseverance. As you bring your heart into alignment with these, you will find His mercy abundant, sufficient, and accessible.

So lift your eyes to the heavens, just as the psalmist did. Tell God your need. Wait with a steadfast, humble heart. Trust that His mercy will not fail. This is the invitation of Psalm 123: not only to survive contempt and scorn, but to thrive in the knowledge that the One enthroned in heaven hears, cares, and responds with boundless mercy to those who cry out to Him.

Let your dependency deepen your relationship, and position you to receive mercy again and again. God's throne is called the throne of mercy for a reason. All who come in faith and humility will find it overflowing, now and always.

Chapter 6

Psalm 124: Praise For Rescue From Enemies.

1 "Had it not been the Lord who was on our side,"
Let Israel say,
2 "Had it not been the Lord who was on our side
When people rose up against us,
3 Then they would have swallowed us alive,
When their anger was kindled against us;
4 Then the waters would have flooded over us,
The stream would have [a]swept over our souls;
5 Then the raging waters would have [b]swept over our souls."
6 Blessed be the Lord,
Who has not given us [c]to be torn by their teeth.
7 Our souls have escaped like a bird from the trapper's snare;
The snare is broken and we have escaped.
8 Our help is in the name of the Lord,
Who made heaven and earth.

Psalm 124 stands as one of scripture's most vivid declarations of God's intervention in the face of overwhelming adversity. Whether you're reading it as a seasoned believer looking for renewed faith or as a seeker longing for hope, the psalm's message is as fresh and powerful today as it was thousands of years ago. By exploring its imagery, context, and practical lessons, we gain not only insight into ancient Israel's experience but also tools to interpret and apply its truths to our own lives.

We approach the scriptures as God's living word—relevant, empowering, and meant to shape our daily lives. When we study the psalms, like Psalm 124, we're not just reading ancient poetry; we're listening for God's voice, searching for wisdom, and being changed in the process. Psalm 124, in particular, stands out as both a historical reflection and a vivid, living picture of God's constant protection.

What happens when overwhelming storms threaten to sweep you away, when enemies surround you, and escape seems impossible? These are not just questions for desperate people—they're part of the human experience. Psalm 124 steps into these moments with a resounding answer: our help comes from the Lord.

Let's examine the structure of Psalm 124. The psalm opens with a repeated refrain: "If the Lord had not been on our side." This isn't mere rhetoric; it's an invitation to imagine what would have happened if God had not intervened. The psalmist uses powerful imagery—floods and raging waters—to depict chaos and disaster. These are more than poetic devices; they represent real threats, moments when defeat seemed certain.

Verses 6-8 shift the imagery to that of rescue: prey escaping a predator and a bird freed from the snare of the fowler. The metaphor is striking—the fowler's trap is cunning, expertly designed, and impossible to escape by human effort alone. Yet, the snare is broken. The psalmist's declaration, "Our help is in the name of the Lord, who made heaven and earth," grounds the entire message: survival and victory are never by our own might, but by the decisive action of the Almighty.

Understanding the historical context deepens our appreciation for this psalm. Psalm 124 is one of the Songs of Ascents, traditionally sung by Israelites journeying to Jerusalem. Many scholars attribute it to King David, who penned it out of his own experience—surrounded by enemies, saved repeatedly by God. Others suggest it could have been sung by the Israelites returning from Babylonian exile, again marking a moment of miraculous deliverance. Either way, the message is timeless: every generation faces threats that would engulf them, but God's protection prevails.

The humility of David's declaration is especially significant given his reputation. David wasn't just a poet; he was a formidable warrior, surrounded by mighty men who accomplished legendary feats. Yet, he insists that victory comes not from human strength or strategy, but from God alone. Psalm 127:1 echoes this: "Unless the Lord builds the house, the builders labor in vain." No matter how skilled or prepared we are, our efforts are futile without God's help.

This isn't a call to passivity. David fought battles, trained his men, and led his people, but his faith was in God's unfailing power. The story of David and Goliath underlines this—David faced a giant not with superior weapons, but with trust in the Lord. "The battle is the Lord's," he declared, and it was God's intervention that brought victory.

The metaphor of the snare of the fowler carries a personal message for anyone who's ever felt trapped—by mistakes, by sin, by circumstances beyond their control. Sometimes, as the psalm suggests, it's not just our enemies but our own failures that ensnare us. Still, God's mercy is greater. As Isaiah 49:24-25 promises, even "lawful captives" can be set free; God redeems not just the innocent, but those who have brought trouble upon themselves. Through Christ, whose blood "speaks better things than the blood of Abel," deliverance is possible for all, regardless of the reason for captivity.

Deliverance starts with recognizing our need for help and calling out to God. Psalm 50:15 makes it clear: "Call upon Me in the day of trouble; I will deliver you." This is not a promise reserved for the blameless; it's rooted in God's mercy, not our righteousness. Lamentations 3:22-23 reminds us that God's compassion is new every morning—His faithfulness never runs out.

The life of David, and the story embedded in Psalm 124, teach us a crucial lesson: even the strongest, most capable among us are ultimately dependent on God. Without Him, all our readiness and effort fall short. With Him, every snare can be broken, every enemy overcome, and every seemingly impossible situation turned around.

So what should we take away from our study of Psalm 124? First, rest in God's sufficiency. Acknowledge your limits, and like the psalmist, declare,

"Our help is in the name of the Lord." Second, call on God in the day of trouble—don't wait until you've exhausted every other option. Third, cultivate gratitude by remembering past deliverances. Gratitude strengthens faith, making it easier to trust God for future battles.

Psalm 124 is more than a song of ancient victory. It's a living testament—a reminder that God's protection is not just a story from the past, but a present reality. No matter the depth of the waters, the strength of the enemy, or the intricacy of the snare, God is able to deliver. As you lean on Him, you will find the snare broken and your soul set free, soaring like a bird released from the fowler's trap.

In the end, the message of Psalm 124 is clear: apart from God's intervention, we are helpless against the forces that threaten us. But with Him on our side, no enemy can stand, and every snare can be shattered. This is the enduring truth and hope that Psalm 124 offers us all.

Chapter 7

Psalm 125: The Lord Surrounds His People.

1 Those who trust in the Lord
Are like Mount Zion, which cannot be moved but remains forever.
2 As the mountains surround Jerusalem,
So the Lord surrounds His people
From this time and forever.
3 For the scepter of wickedness will not rest upon the [a]land of the righteous,
So that the righteous will not extend their hands to do wrong.
4 Do good, Lord, to those who are good
And to those who are upright in their hearts.
5 But as for those who turn aside to their crooked ways,
The Lord will lead them away with those who practice injustice.
Peace be upon Israel.

Psalm 125 stands as one of the Bible's most stirring portraits of divine protection and unshakable faith. It is a beacon for anyone longing for unshakeable security and peace amid life's uncertainties.. Like Psalm 122, it draws us to Jerusalem, where a pilgrim beholds the city's safety and security—a scene starkly different from the contempt encountered in Psalm 123. With God's help (as Psalm 124 reminds us), Jerusalem reappears, not merely as a city but as a metaphor for spiritual stability. The psalmist likens those who trust in the Lord to Mount Zion itself: immovable, enduring, and surrounded by mountains that symbolize God's lasting protection.

"What would life look like if you lived completely fearless, unshaken by life's storms, and untouched by the schemes of the wicked?" Psalm 125 answers this question with bold imagery and timeless assurances. "Those who trust in the Lord are like Mount Zion, which cannot be shaken but endures forever" (Psalm 125:1). This verse sets the tone for a psalm that isn't just about hope—it's a blueprint for a life anchored in God's promises. Standing in ancient Jerusalem, one would see the city tucked securely among rugged mountain ranges: the Mount of Olives to the east, Mount Scopus to the north, and other hills forming a natural fortress. In times of war, these mountains were the city's first line of defense, providing stability and protection when enemies threatened. The psalmist chooses this setting deliberately, using it as a vivid spiritual metaphor: just as Jerusalem is shielded by mountains, so God surrounds His people, both now and forever.

This protection is not fragile or fleeting; it is, as the psalmist insists, "eternal and unconquerable." Trusting God wholeheartedly activates this promise. True trust is not half-hearted. It's not keeping God as a backup plan. It's saying, "God, You are my only option. Without You, I am nothing." This kind of trust invites God's presence and power in a way that nothing else can. Abraham's willingness to sacrifice Isaac (Genesis 22) is the scriptural model for this kind of faith—no plan B, only utter reliance on God's integrity.

Psalm 125 also carries a profound warning and a promise: "The scepter of the wicked will not rest on the land allotted to the righteous" (Psalm 125:3). God is deeply concerned that His people not fall into the ways of the ungodly. He opposes wickedness, not only to protect His people but to preserve their holiness. This psalm, like so many others, pulses with themes of righteousness, justice, and the hope that peace (shalom) will ultimately prevail.

But how do these promises play out in real life? The answer lies in the alignment of the heart—a heart in tune with God's will and voice. "O LORD, do good to those who are good, whose hearts are in tune with you" (Psalm 125:4). When your heart is attuned to God, you're able to hear His voice even above life's noise. Sometimes, this means receiving guidance that protects you from unseen dangers—a quiet prompting not to take a certain route or make a particular decision. Billy Graham often recounted such moments of inward leading, instances when God's guidance protected him from harm and propelled him toward greater purpose.

This is not passive trust; it is an active, purposeful alignment. It means listening, obeying, and depending on God's wisdom in all things. When you live this way, God's favor and protection surround you as surely as the mountains surround Jerusalem. The psalmist's imagery isn't just poetic; it's a reality for those who trust and obey.

Yet Psalm 125's message goes even further. God's children are not only protected—they are called to rule. Dominion is not restricted to political office but extends to every sphere: wealth, justice, culture, family, business, and the arts. Too often, believers have ceded these areas to the wicked, resulting in corruption, injustice, and ungodliness. This is not God's will. His intent, from the beginning, was for His children to exercise dominion on earth (Genesis 1:26). Christ's death and resurrection restored this authority, seating believers with Him "in heavenly places" (Ephesians 2:6).

This spiritual hierarchy is clear: God as supreme authority, believers next (seated with Christ), angels serving believers, demons subject to Christ and to believers, and, finally, the wicked and unbelievers at the lowest rank. When Christians abdicate their authority—when they fail to understand or act on this spiritual ranking—the wicked rule by default. Psalm 125 declares that this is not the way it should be. "The scepter of the wicked shall not rest on the land allotted to the righteous," not just as a promise, but as a call to action.

Believers must rise and take their place in every area of life: in government, by voting, running for office, and leading with justice; in business, by building enterprises that honor God; in the judiciary, by pursuing justice in line with God's principles; in culture and media, by upholding righteousness and creative excellence. This is the real meaning of kingdom dominion.

None of this is possible without wholehearted trust in God. As the psalmist writes, only those who trust God wholly are surrounded by His protection and empowered to walk boldly into every calling. Trusting God means making Him your only option and living in total obedience. When you do, He moves mightily, shields you from evil, and ensures that the wicked cannot prevail.

Psalm 125, therefore, is more than a song of comfort—it is a call to action. It reminds believers not to leave their destiny in the hands of the wicked. Instead, it urges them to know their authority, reclaim their dominion, and rule in every area of life. The world will only see justice, peace, and godliness prevail when God's people step into their ordained positions.

In summary, Psalm 125 teaches three interwoven truths: first, that trusting God brings unshakable protection, as sure as the mountains around Jerusalem; second, that believers are called to rule and must not let the wicked dominate; and third, that a heart in tune with God hears His guidance and walks in His blessings. These lessons form the foundation of a life marked by divine security, purpose, and steadfast faith.

To trust God is to anchor your life in His steadfast presence. It means making Him your only option, trusting His integrity, and aligning your heart with His will. When you do, you step into a life shielded from evil, empowered to bring about justice and righteousness, and guided by the very hand of God. The psalm concludes with a prayer for peace upon Israel—a hope that God's kingdom purposes will be realized and that His shalom will rule in every heart.

Psalm 125 is a call to wholehearted trust, courageous dominion, and unwavering alignment with God. As you meditate on these truths, may you be inspired to trust Him fully, rise to your calling, and live each day wrapped in His unshakeable protection and peace.

May the truths of Psalm 125 inspire you to trust God wholeheartedly, align your heart with His, and step confidently into the fullness of His protection, favor, and calling—today and always.

Chapter 8

Psalm 126: Thanksgiving For Return From Captivity.

1When the Lord brought back [a]the captives of Zion,
We were like those who dream.
2 Then our mouth was filled with laughter
And our tongue with joyful shouting;
Then they said among the nations,
"The Lord has done great things for them."
3 The Lord has done great things for us;
We are joyful.
4 Restore our fortunes, Lord,
As the [b]streams in the [c]South.
5 Those who sow in tears shall harvest with joyful shouting.
6 One who goes here and there weeping, carrying his bag of seed,
Shall indeed come again with a shout of joy, bringing his sheaves with him.

Restoration in Psalm 126 teaches that the true miracle isn't just physical rebuilding, but hearts turning back to God. Spiritual renewal always takes precedence. The psalmist prays, "Restore our fortunes, O Lord," not merely for comfort, but for revival that honors God's name among all nations. This longing is echoed in other scriptures—Psalm 85, the story of Elijah, the journey of Joseph, Job, and even Paul's words in Romans 1. In each, restoration is tied to forgiveness, spiritual health, and ultimately, God's glory. Think of Abraham, waiting half a century for a child. He and Sarah longed, prayed, and despaired—then God delivered not just a son, but the child of promise, through whom nations would be blessed. That's the nature of

God's restoration: it surpasses human expectations. The Israelites returning from exile, Job receiving double after his losses, Joseph moving from prison to prime minister overnight—each story carries the same signature. When

God restores, it's unmistakable, often leaving us speechless. The joy wipes away tears of many years in an instant.

Psalm 126 stands as a powerful meditation on restoration, joy, and the unmistakable work of God in the lives of His people. It reflects on God restoring Zion's fortunes, filling mouths with laughter and tongues with joy. The psalm begins with gratitude for past restorations and moves into a prayer for future blessing: "Restore our fortunes, O Lord."

Restoration in the biblical sense is never just about recovering what was lost. When God restores, it's overflow—joy beyond what anyone could imagine, and glory that points unmistakably to Him. We see this in the Israelites' return from exile, an event so miraculous that it felt like a dream: "Our mouths were filled with laughter, our tongues with songs of joy." The restoration was so profound that even the nations noticed and said, "The Lord has done great things for them."

The pattern repeats throughout scripture. Abraham waited decades for a child, and when the promise was fulfilled, it wasn't just any child, but Isaac—the child through whom nations would be blessed. Job, after losing everything, was restored with double what he had before. Joseph, betrayed and imprisoned for years, went to bed one night a prisoner and woke up the next day as Prime Minister of Egypt. Each story reveals a God who not only restores, but multiplies, surprises, and brings glory to Himself through the transformation.

This theme is found in other psalms, such as Psalm 85, and in the stories of Elijah, Paul, and even Nelson Mandela. In each case, restoration comes not merely as a personal blessing, but as a testimony to the world—an undeniable work of God that ignites hope and faith in others.

A key insight from Psalm 126 is that true restoration is spiritual renewal. The heart of the matter is not just rebuilding walls or recovering possessions, but having hearts turn back to God. The psalmist's joy is rooted in forgiveness and a renewed relationship with the Lord, not just outward change. When God restores, it's about laughter and praise replacing weeping and tears, and people's lives becoming living testimonies of His faithfulness.

Evangelism and God's work in the world are ultimately aimed at this: that God's name would be honored among all nations. Paul's words in Romans 1 echo this sentiment—the gospel spreads for God's name's sake, so that others would experience His restorative joy.

Restoration almost never happens instantly. Let's be clear, it can happy instantaneously as we are reminded in several places in the Bible. However, there is a steady stream of places where it doesn't happen instantly as well. The journey from loss to laughter typically involves a season of waiting, testing, and planting seeds in faith. The psalmist notes, "Those who sow in tears will reap with songs of joy." Behind every "miracle out of nowhere" lies a story of perseverance, obedience, and often, silent suffering and trust. Consider Joseph. Most people see the glory, but few ask about the story. Years of betrayal, slavery, false accusation, and loneliness preceded his sudden rise. Job's loss was almost unimaginable, yet his trust in God was unwavering: "Though He slay me, yet will I trust Him." David, anointed king as a youth, spent years on the run, refusing to take shortcuts to the throne, and honoring even those who persecuted him.

The pattern is clear: God's restorations nearly always follow a season of preparation and waiting. What the world calls "miracles" are often the fruit of faithfulness, obedience, and trust through trials.

So, how do we posture ourselves during these seasons of waiting? How do we keep faith alive while longing for God to turn our weeping into rejoicing?

1. Hold on to God's Word with Trust and Peace

The promises of God are the anchor during seasons of waiting. Like Abraham, we are called to trust in God's "I will." Find scriptures that address your need, speak them daily, and let them shape your prayers. Keep peace in your heart, trusting God's timing. Even Jesus wept, but He never doubted. Let your tears water the seeds of faith you are planting.

2. Practice Hospitality and Kindness

Restoration often arrives through the ordinary kindnesses we show along the way. Abraham's hospitality to strangers ushered in the fulfillment of God's promise. Joseph served faithfully in prison, interpreting dreams for others even while awaiting his own breakthrough. The Bible encourages us: "Do not forget to show hospitality to strangers, for by so doing some people have shown hospitality to angels without knowing it" (Hebrews 13:2). Your kindness and faithfulness in the waiting season are seeds God will remember.

3. Keep Silent Under Mockery and Pressure

Seasons of waiting can be marked by mockery or misunderstanding. "Where is your God?" people may ask. Jesus, when mocked on the cross, entrusted His vindication to the Father. Sometimes, silence is the best answer. Let God handle shame and ridicule; He alone gets the glory when restoration comes.

4. Consistency in Prayer and Worship

It's easy to grow weary in prayer during long waits, but this is when prayer becomes most crucial. Prayer aligns your heart with God; worship shifts your focus from the problem to God's greatness. "Those who sow in tears will reap with songs of joy." Worship is your song of joy before the harvest comes. Restoration often follows seasons of earnest prayer and sincere worship.

5. Resist Depression and Negative Suggestions

The enemy will do everything to make you believe waiting on God is pointless. Quotes like "Maybe God has forgotten me" or "Maybe I'm not worthy" can creep in. Fight these lies with gratitude and remembrance of God's past faithfulness. Even Jesus on the cross, and Job in his despair, held on to trust in God. Restoration is a process, but the end result is always joy. No matter how long you've waited or how much you've lost, remember: when God restores, it's always more than you imagined. It's never just about you; it's about those who witness your transformation and see God's hand at work. The story of Nebuchadnezzar reminds us to give God the glory.

Restoration is meant to make God's greatness known.

Are you waiting for God's restoration in your life? Hold on to hope. Like the Israelites, Job, and Joseph, your season of laughter and joy is coming. The journey may be through tears, but the harvest is joy and a testimony that amazes the world.

Waiting on God for restoration demands trust, persistence, and faith in His timing. The stories of Joseph, Job, and David, as well as the testimony of Psalm 126, teach us that waiting is not a wasteland. Restoration requires planting seeds of faith, obedience, and service, even when you feel empty or forgotten. We see that restoration almost always comes after a season of preparation and perseverance. The journey may be marked by tears, doubts, and trials, but the end is always joy—so overwhelming, it feels like a dream.

No matter how long you've waited or how much you've lost, keep sowing in faith, keep walking in obedience, and keep trusting His perfect timing. When God restores, it's like a dream; it will be more than you can imagine— full of joy, overflowing with glory, and rich with testimonies that declare His faithfulness to the world. So keep sowing, keep praying, keep praising, and keep trusting His perfect timing. When God restores, it's never just for you—it's a testimony to His faithfulness that draws others to Him. And then, like those who returned to Zion, you'll find your mouth filled with laughter and your heart brimming with songs of joy, declaring to all: "The Lord has done great things for us, and we are filled with joy."

Chapter 9

Psalm 127: Prosperity Comes From The Lord.

1 Unless the Lord builds a house,
They who build it labor in vain;
Unless the Lord guards a city,
The watchman stays awake in vain.
2 It is futile for you to rise up early,
To [a]stay up late,
To eat the bread of painful labor;
This is how He gives to His beloved sleep.
3 Behold, children are a [b]gift of the Lord,
The fruit of the womb is a reward.
4 Like arrows in the hand of a warrior,
So are the children of one's youth.
5 Blessed is the man whose quiver is full of them;
They will not be ashamed
When they speak with their enemies in the gate.

We continue our examination of the Songs of Ascents, focusing specifically on Psalms 127. However, we will also examine Psalms 128 as both Psalms 127 and 128 are undoubtedly intertwined. In a world that often champions self-sufficiency, ambition, and self-determination—telling us to "trust in yourself" or that we are the masters of our destinies—these psalms offer a profoundly countercultural perspective. While independence and ambition might sound empowering, they can easily tip into a burdensome self-sufficiency, causing people to carry loads they were never meant to bear.

Psalm 127, attributed to Solomon, stands as a beacon of wisdom for anyone tempted to rely solely on their own strength. It reminds us that, no matter how smart, hardworking, or resourceful we are, our bodies and minds are limited; apart from God, our efforts cannot produce lasting fruit.

The central message of Psalm 127 slices through the cultural noise: "Unless the LORD builds the house, the builders labor in vain. Unless the LORD watches over the city, the guards stand watch in vain." These words point out the futility of human effort without God's involvement. It's not a call to laziness—diligence and hard work are still important—but a reminder that success, security, and blessing flow from God, not from our striving. This psalm balances diligence with dependence, showing that true security and fulfillment come from resting in God's provision.

History is full of reminders that human confidence alone is not enough. The story of the Titanic, hailed as "unsinkable," ended in disaster despite human ingenuity and technological prowess—highlighting that no amount of planning guarantees success when God is pushed to the margins. Scripture echoes this repeatedly: "Many are the plans in a person's heart, but it is the LORD's purpose that prevails" (Proverbs 19:21); "Apart from me you can do nothing" (John 15:5). The lesson is clear: self-reliance is both prideful and shortsighted. When we trust in ourselves alone, we not only risk failure, but we also miss out on God's greater purposes for our lives.

Psalm 127's imagery of building and guarding is deeply practical. Building a house symbolizes our efforts, ambitions, and plans; watching over a city stands for our attempts to protect and secure what we've gained. Yet the psalmist insists that without God's blessing, both activities are ultimately in vain. This is not a denial of human responsibility—God expects us to work. But it's a call to work with humility, acknowledging our dependence on Him for every outcome.

This principle extends beyond work to the family. Psalm 127 declares, "Children are a heritage from the LORD, offspring a reward from him. Like arrows in the hands of a warrior are children born in one's youth." Just as our work is ultimately blessed by God, so too are our families. Children are not burdens or liabilities, but gifts entrusted to us by God. This perspective transforms the way we view and care for them—not as products of human achievement, but as part of God's gracious plan. Parenting, then, becomes an act of stewardship, requiring wisdom, strength, and patience that only God can provide.

The New Testament reframes the material blessings of family and work as spiritual blessings in Christ, urging us to see our daily lives through the lens of God's ongoing provision and purpose. As we trust God with our labor and our families, we are freed from relentless striving and anxiety. We learn that rest is not a sign of laziness but of faith—God "grants sleep to those he loves." By surrendering our plans and anxieties to Him, we enter into a peace that surpasses understanding (Philippians 4:6-7).

Psalm 128 builds on these truths, emphasizing the blessings that flow from personal devotion and obedience to God. It acknowledges the reality of a broken world—sometimes, hard work does not yield the hoped-for results. Yet, it affirms that a life built on faith and obedience is the way to experience God's enduring favor. Both psalms trace these themes back to Genesis 1, reminding us of God's original design and purpose for work and family. They invite us to work diligently, but always with the awareness that ultimate success is God's to give.

This examination of Psalms 127 and 128 brings us to a pivotal application for today: how do we live out these ancient lessons in our modern context? Start by surrendering your plans to God in prayer each day, seeking His guidance in every decision. Let go of the anxiety produced by self-reliance, and trust that God's plans for you far exceed anything you could accomplish on your own. As Proverbs 3:5-6 encourages, "Trust in the LORD with all your heart and lean not on your own understanding; in all your ways submit to him, and he will make your paths straight."

Rest in the knowledge that it is not by strength that one prevails (1 Samuel 2:9), but by God's grace. Whether in your career, your family, or your daily struggles, remember that God is the builder and protector of all that truly matters. When we trust Him, our lives gain meaning that endures beyond our own abilities, and the blessings we enjoy become legacies that impact generations to come.

The call of both Psalm 127 and 128 is clear and timeless: Trust God and let Him lead. Relinquish the burdens of self-sufficiency, and discover the peace, purpose, and fulfillment that only He can provide. His blessing, not our striving, determines the outcome. When we surrender both our work and our families to Him, we find the peace, rest, and security that self-reliance can never deliver. God is the builder and protector of all that truly matters. Let Him lead, and your life will bear fruit that endures.

As you reflect on these psalms, remember: Pursuing life independently of God is futile. Blessings come from Him alone. Trust, surrender, and let Him build your life.

"Trust in the Lord with all your heart and lean not on your own understanding." (Proverbs 3:5)

Chapter 10

Psalm 128: Blessedness Of The Fear Of The Lord.

1 Blessed is everyone who fears the Lord,
Who walks in His ways.
2 When you eat the fruit of the labor of your hands,
You will be happy and it will go well for you.
3 Your wife will be like a fruitful vine
[a] Within your house,
Your children like olive plants
Around your table.
4 Behold, for so shall a man
Who fears the Lord be blessed.
5 The Lord bless you from Zion,
And may you see the prosperity of Jerusalem all the days of your life.
6 Indeed, may you see your children's children.
Peace be upon Israel!

We continue our journey through the Songs of Ascents, pausing now to reflect deeply on Psalms 128 using its connection with Psalms 127 to develop a larger theme. These psalms, Psalms 128 and 127, invite us to consider what it means to live a life dedicated to God in a world shaped by brokenness, as we wait between Christ's redemption and His return. They contain an eternal secret, hidden in plain sight: real blessing—spiritual, material, and familial—flows out of a life centered on the fear of God. These psalms offer deep wisdom about work, family, personal devotion, and the enduring blessings that come from centering life on the fear of God.

Both psalms echo the themes of Genesis 1, pointing back to God's original design for work and family. They remind us that our toil and relationships are meant to be infused with purpose and blessing when lived under God's sovereignty. The New Testament deepens this, reframing material blessings as spiritual riches in Christ, yet still calling us to continuous trust and obedience.

The psalmists also connect personal piety to the health of the wider community. "May you see the prosperity of Jerusalem all the days of your life," Psalm 128 declares, linking household faithfulness to national well-being. As Proverbs 14:34 says, "Righteousness exalts a nation, but sin condemns any people." The spiritual integrity of families shapes the destiny of societies. Consider King Hezekiah, whose faithfulness brought peace and prosperity to Judah by turning the nation's heart back to God.

Harmony at home is not accidental but cultivated by intentional, godly living. When every family member lives with reverence for God, mutual respect and love flourish, and the home becomes a sanctuary of peace—even in a chaotic world. As Isaiah 26:3 promises, "You will keep in perfect peace those whose minds are steadfast, because they trust in you." The blessings of fearing God ripple outward, fostering not just individual contentment but also communal welfare and national peace.

In sum, Psalms 127 and 128 paint a vivid picture of the blessings that flow from a life centered on the fear of the Lord. This is not about being afraid, but about honoring, trusting, and submitting to God's authority. Those who do so experience the fruit of their labor, harmony in their homes, and the assurance of generational blessings. Their influence extends beyond their own households, contributing to the prosperity and peace of their communities and nations.

These psalms encourage us to reorient our lives, moving from independence to a God-centered approach—knowing that true peace, meaning, and lasting blessing come only from Him. In a world often marked by strife and uncertainty, the fear of the Lord offers the pathway to contentment and enduring reward. May we all strive to walk in the fear of the Lord, reaping the abundant rewards He so graciously provides.

As Proverbs 3:5-6 reminds us: "Trust in the Lord with all your heart and lean not on your own understanding." In doing so, our labor, our families, and even our nations find their truest peace and purpose.

Psalm 127 sets the stage by highlighting the futility of human effort apart from God's presence. "Unless the Lord builds the house, those who build it labor in vain." This opening line crystallizes the message: true success— in work, family, and community—depends on divine assistance. The text touches on the importance of hard work and the value of rest, with sleep serving as a symbol of trust in God's provision. The psalm also celebrates children as a heritage and reward from the Lord, reinforcing Old Testament themes that link prosperity with divine favor.

But the message doesn't stop at material success. The New Testament perspective reframes these Old Testament blessings, pointing to deeper spiritual realities in Christ. While diligent work is good, the ultimate fruitfulness of our labor—be it in career or family—rests in God's hands. This shifts the focus from independence to dependence, from self-reliance to God-reliance. As Proverbs 3:5-6 encourages: "Trust in the Lord with all your heart and lean not on your own understanding."

If Psalm 127 establishes the need for God's involvement, Psalm 128 explores the heart posture that invites His blessing: the fear of the Lord. This is not dread or terror, but a deep reverence for God's holiness, power, and love—a willingness to align one's life with His will, trust His wisdom, and walk in His ways. Job offers a powerful example of this truth; even in the darkest trials, his reverence for God brought restoration and multiplied blessings.

Psalm 128 promises that those who fear God and walk in His ways will "eat the fruit of their labor," experience peace at home, and see generational blessings. This vision is more than personal prosperity; it encompasses happiness, fulfillment, and stability—a holistic prosperity that transcends mere material gain. Solomon, the wisest man in history, declared, "The fear of the Lord is the beginning of wisdom" (Proverbs 9:10), linking reverence for God to the kind of wisdom that leads to lasting prosperity.

The imagery in Psalm 128 is rich and evocative. A wife is described as a "fruitful vine within your house"—a symbol of abundance, vitality, and enduring love. Children are "like olive shoots around your table"—promising growth, stability, and generational continuity. These metaphors point to the power of a godly home. When family members honor God, their relationships are marked by love, mutual respect, and peace, creating a sanctuary where each person can thrive.

Such households don't emerge by accident. They are cultivated through intentional, godly living. The example of Aquila and Priscilla in the New Testament demonstrates how shared reverence for God can make a home a center for spiritual growth and community impact (Acts 18:26). The story of Abraham, too, shows how one person's faith can establish a legacy of blessing for many generations (Genesis 22:15-18).

Psalm 128 does not limit its vision to the nuclear family. The blessings of those who fear God overflow to the community and, by extension, the nation. "May you see the prosperity of Jerusalem all the days of your life." This verse connects personal piety to national flourishing, echoing Proverbs 14:34: "Righteousness exalts a nation, but sin condemns any people." When families honor God, their collective integrity contributes to the wellbeing and peace of the broader society.

The reign of King Hezekiah in 2 Chronicles 31:20-21 offers a historical illustration: his personal devotion and the people's return to the fear of God led to prosperity and peace for Judah. The health of a nation is deeply tied to the spiritual integrity and reverence of its people.

"May you live to see your children's children." This blessing of longevity is about more than lifespan—it's about witnessing the transmission of faith and values across generations. Proverbs 17:6 captures it beautifully: "Children's children are a crown to the aged." Families rooted in the fear of the Lord create a stable, moral fabric that sustains communities and nations through time.

The psalm concludes with a prayer for shalom—wholeness, tranquility, and welfare. This peace is the fruit of righteousness and reverence for God, extending from individuals and families to the nation at large. Isaiah 32:17 affirms: "The fruit of that righteousness will be peace; its effect will be quietness and confidence forever." In a world often marked by instability and strife, the fear of God offers a secure anchor and the promise of enduring contentment.

The psalm closes with a vision of enduring legacy: "May you live to see your children's children—peace be on Israel." This isn't just about personal longevity but about witnessing the perpetuation of godliness and blessing through generations. Proverbs 17:6 affirms, "Children's children are a crown to the aged." When families are rooted in the fear of God, faith and stability are passed down, weaving a moral fabric that upholds society.

Peace—shalom—in this context means wholeness, welfare, and tranquility. It is the fruit of righteousness (Isaiah 32:17) and is attainable when reverence for God permeates the lives of individuals, families, and nations. Such peace stands in stark contrast to the anxiety and instability that mark so much of modern life.

Together, Psalms 127 and 128 form a powerful blueprint for living. They remind us that the foundation of a blessed, prosperous, and peaceful life is not found in frantic striving or self-sufficiency, but in humble dependence on God and a heart that truly reveres Him. Work and family are sacred callings, but their true fruitfulness is a gift from God. The blessings that flow from honoring Him reach far beyond our own lives, shaping future generations and even the destiny of nations.

May we all strive to walk in the fear of the Lord, trusting Him with our labor, our families, and our future—reaping the abundant rewards He so graciously provides, and becoming conduits of His blessing in our communities and world.

The below plan is simply an example plan that could be used to jumpstart your small group. While this plan is meant to be enacted as part of the local congregation, it does not have to be limited to that scope. It simply could be started as a side project by any Christian group that is operating from a home.

Chapter 11

Psalm 129: Prayer For The Overthrow Of Zion's Enemies.

1 "[a]Many times they have attacked me from my youth up,"
Let Israel say,
2 "[b]Many times they have attacked me from my youth up;
Yet they have not prevailed against me.
3 The plowers plowed upon my back;
They lengthened their furrows."
4 The Lord is righteous;
He has cut up the ropes of the wicked.
5 May all who hate Zion
Be put to shame and turned backward;
6 May they be like grass upon the housetops,
Which withers before it [c]grows up;
7 With which the harvester does not fill his [d]hand,
Or the binder of sheaves his [e]arms;
8 Nor do those who pass by say,
"The blessing of the Lord be upon you;
We bless you in the name of the Lord."

The journey of faith is never without its trials. Life is often marked by seasons of hardship, affliction, and persecution, a reality reflected throughout Scripture and poignantly captured in Psalm 129. Known as one of the "Songs of Ascents," this psalm does more than recount the historical struggles of Israel—it offers timeless encouragement for all who endure trials for their faith. It is both a lament over repeated affliction and a declaration of God's

51

unchanging power to deliver—a theme just as relevant for believers today. In this Psalm, the psalmist gives voice to Israel's long and painful history of suffering at the hands of their enemies, beginning with the phrase, "Many a time have they afflicted me from my youth, may Israel now say." This refrain echoes the deep scars left by oppression, not only on Israel but on all those who walk in faith.

Yet, Psalm 129 is not just a historical account; it's a living word of encouragement for anyone enduring hardship. Each verse invites us to remember that, while the wounds of persecution may run deep, they are also evidence of survival. The marks left by affliction are not signs of defeat, but reminders of God's delivering power. As the psalmist reflects, the scars from past trials are trophies of God's faithfulness—proof that, though afflicted, God's people have not been overcome.

This enduring affliction is not unique to ancient Israel. Every believer who has faced hostility or adversity because of their faith can relate to the struggles described here. From the Israelites' bondage in Egypt, through battles in the Promised Land, to the church's suffering in every age, God's people have always encountered opposition. The psalmist's words, "Yet they have not prevailed against me," serve as a rallying cry for all who endure persecution, affirming that survival itself is a victory.

Psalm 129 opens with a collective voice: "Many a time have they afflicted me from my youth, may Israel now say." The psalmist remembers the long history of Israel's suffering, from Egyptian bondage to ongoing opposition in the Promised Land. These afflictions were not unique to Israel; every believer who faces hostility for their faith can relate to the trials described.
The psalmist employs vivid imagery: "The plowers plowed upon my back; they made long their furrows." This metaphor evokes the beatings and oppression that left deep marks—scars signifying both pain and survival. Yet, these scars are not tokens of defeat. Rather, they testify to victories won and chains broken by God's sustaining power. Just as the Israelites' scars told stories of God's deliverance, so do the scars of every believer who endures for God's sake.

We are reminded that the journey of faith is not a promise of immunity from affliction, but a testimony to God's faithfulness through it. Enduring persecution may leave marks, but they serve as proof of a God who never abandons His people. As David declared after past deliverances, "The Lord who rescued me from the paw of the lion and the paw of the bear will rescue me from the hand of this Philistine" (1 Samuel 17:37). Past victories are the foundation for future faith.

Central to Psalm 129 is the confident declaration in verse 4: "But the LORD is righteous; he has cut the cords of the wicked." Despite all the pain inflicted, the psalmist affirms that God's righteousness secures deliverance for His people. The cords represent the chains of oppression, control, and bondage—whether inflicted by human enemies or spiritual forces.

God's intervention is not a matter of chance. "The LORD is good," the psalmist affirms. His goodness is constant, not dictated by circumstances. James 1:17 assures us, "Every good and perfect gift is from above, coming down from the Father of the heavenly lights, who does not change like shifting shadows." God's deliverance is motivated by His perfect love and unwavering character.

The phrase "He has cut the cords" is written in the past tense, highlighting the certainty and completeness of God's deliverance. Often, God's work precedes our full understanding—what appears as persistent bondage may already be broken in the spiritual realm. Our deliverance is not delayed, but divinely appointed, for "He has made everything beautiful in its time" (Ecclesiastes 3:11).

Scripture is filled with reminders of God's power to break every chain: He delivered Israel from Egypt, destroyed Jericho's walls, freed Paul and Silas from prison. Isaiah 10:27 promises, "The yoke shall be destroyed because of the anointing." In each case, the cords of affliction were decisively severed. For believers, this deliverance is ultimately secured in Jesus Christ, who "disarmed the powers and authorities, triumphing over them by the cross" (Colossians 2:15).

Affliction, then, is not evidence of abandonment. Rather, it is the backdrop against which God's glory and faithfulness are revealed. When enduring persecution, we can declare with confidence: "Many a time have they afflicted me from my youth, yet they have not prevailed against me."

The psalm transitions from lament and remembrance to a prayer for justice: "Let them all be confounded and turned back that hate Zion. Let them be as the grass upon the housetops, which withereth afore it groweth up." (Psalm 129:5–6)

This prayer is not motivated by personal vengeance, but by a longing for God's righteousness to prevail. The enemies of God's people are those who "hate Zion"—who oppose God's kingdom, purposes, and people. Their hatred is active, seeking to destroy what aligns with God's will. Psalm 2 describes this as the nations' futile rebellion against the Lord and His anointed.

The psalmist uses a striking metaphor: grass on a rooftop. In ancient Israel, shallow layers of soil on flat roofs allowed grass to sprout quickly but wither under the sun before it matured. This image underscores the fleeting nature of the wicked's power. Their schemes may appear threatening, but they are insubstantial and doomed to fail. As Job 8:11–13 and Psalm 37:2 remind us, the prosperity of the wicked is brief, and their end is certain.

Scripture calls believers to pray for their enemies (Matthew 5:44), yet it also gives precedent for calling on God to execute justice. Praying the decrees of Psalm 129 is not an act of hatred, but an expression of trust in God's sovereignty. "Do not take revenge... but leave room for God's wrath," writes Paul in Romans 12:19. When we entrust our struggles to Him, we rest in the assurance that He sees every injustice and will act in His perfect time (Revelation 6:10).

The decrees of Psalm 129 point to the ultimate victory God promises His people. Though enemies rage, they cannot prevail against those whom God has chosen to bless. The outcome is already decided in Christ: "In all these things we are more than conquerors through him who loved us" (Romans 8:37).

How, then, should believers respond in seasons of affliction or persecution? Psalm 129 offers practical encouragement:

- **Pray Boldly:** Use the decrees of Psalm 129 as a guide for prayer. Declare that every scheme of the enemy will be confounded and turned back.
- **Trust God's Justice:** Rest in the knowledge that God sees your struggles and will act on your behalf. His justice may be delayed, but it is never denied.

- **Remember the Fragility of Evil:** When persecution feels overwhelming, recall the image of grass on the rooftop—evil may flourish for a time, but it cannot last.

- **Celebrate Victory:** The battle may be fierce, but God's victory is assured. Find strength in His promises, knowing He has already "cut the cords" of oppression.

- **Reflect on Past Deliverance:** Like David, let past victories fuel your faith for new battles. Thank God for what He has done, and trust Him for what is to come.

Psalm 129 is a profound reminder of God's unwavering power to deliver His people, even in the most trying circumstances. Whether enduring persecution through illness, family crisis, or spiritual attack, the God who delivered Israel stands ready to deliver you. Scripture assures us: "Many are the afflictions of the righteous, but the LORD delivers him out of them all" (Psalm 34:19).

Psalm 129 stands as a rallying cry for all who walk the path of faith amid adversity. It assures us that suffering is never a sign of abandonment, that God's justice will prevail, and that His deliverance is sure. Let this psalm inspire your faith and strengthen your resolve to stand firm in the promises of God. Your enemies will not prosper; their might will dwindle, and God's righteousness will endure. Trust in His deliverance, pray boldly, and rest in the victory already won for you through Christ. In every season of trial, let Psalm 129 be your song of hope.

Chapter 12

Psalm 130: Hope In The Lord's Forgiving Love.

1 Out of the depths I have cried to You, Lord.
2 Lord, hear my voice!
Let Your ears be attentive
To the sound of my pleadings.
3 If You, [a]Lord, were to keep account of guilty deeds,
Lord, who could stand?
4 But there is forgiveness with You,
So that You may be [b]revered.
5 I wait for the Lord, my soul waits,
And I [c]wait for His word.
6 My soul waits in hope for the Lord
More than the watchmen for the morning;
Yes, more than the watchmen for the morning.
7 Israel, wait for the Lord;
For with the Lord there is mercy,
And with Him is abundant redemption.
8 And He will redeem Israel
From all his guilty deeds.

Psalm 130, often called "De Profundis" or "Out of the Depths," stands as one of the most moving prayers in scripture. Its words have echoed through Christian liturgy for centuries, offering comfort to the weary and hope to the repentant. Its enduring power lies in its honest cry for mercy and its unshakeable confidence in God's love and forgiveness.

Psalm 130, known as "De Profundis" or "Out of the Depths," stands as one of the most heartfelt cries for mercy found in scripture—a raw plea rising up from despair and a powerful testimony to God's steadfast love and restoration. Its influence runs deep: Martin Luther called it central to the gospel; John Wesley heard it just days before his own conversion; and it holds a prominent place in the liturgies of the Church of England. At its core, Psalm 130 is about the struggle with sin, the agony of waiting, and the hope that springs from God's unfailing grace.

The psalm is divided into four distinct movements. It opens with a deeply personal plea for mercy, as the psalmist acknowledges both the reality of sin and the extraordinary willingness of God to forgive. "Out of the depths I cry to You, Lord!" (Psalm 130:1) is more than poetic language—it's the honest confession of a soul that's tried every human solution and found them lacking. This sense of "depths" captures the overwhelming nature of life's struggles—whether they stem from guilt, hardship, or despair.

When we find ourselves in these low places—facing financial troubles, health challenges, broken relationships, or haunting guilt—the psalmist's instinct is instructive: he turns not to human help, but straight to God. Human beings, no matter how loving, are limited; even with the best intentions, they cannot always rescue us. By contrast, God hears every cry, responds with mercy, and never delays in fulfilling His promises. The beauty of Psalm 130 is in its assurance that God is not distant or indifferent. He is attentive, ready to forgive, and quick to restore.

This theme is echoed in stories throughout the Bible. After Jesus' crucifixion, Peter and the disciples, overwhelmed by failure and uncertainty, returned to fishing—only to catch nothing until Jesus intervened. Their breakthrough came not from their own expertise, but from obeying the Lord's instruction. This mirrors the lesson of Psalm 130: our efforts, no matter how well-intentioned, cannot replace the need for divine intervention. God often anticipates our needs before we even voice them, preparing a way for deliverance.

A foundational message of Psalm 130 is that God's forgiveness is absolute. "If You, Lord, kept a record of sins, Lord, who could stand?" (Psalm 130:3)

This is not just a rhetorical question—it's a profound truth. Unlike humans, who may struggle to forget past wrongs, God wipes the slate clean. Isaiah 43:25 declares that He remembers our sins no more, and 2 Corinthians 5:19 reminds us that Jesus has already paid the price, so God no longer counts our sins against us. Many believers live under unnecessary guilt, but Psalm 130 insists that through Christ, we are fully forgiven and accepted.

Yet, forgiveness is not a license to ignore God. Instead, it draws us closer, leading to reverence and gratitude. The psalmist says, "But with You there is forgiveness, so that we can, with reverence, serve You." True forgiveness inspires deeper devotion, not complacency. Even when the devil accuses, trying to keep us bound by our past, we can stand firm in the truth that our debt is settled. If you struggle with a guilty conscience or unconfessed sin, Psalm 130 offers comfort: God forgives quickly and completely, and His love is steadfast.

Another crucial aspect of Psalm 130 is the call to patient hope. Verses 5-6 use the image of watchmen waiting for the morning—a vivid picture of anticipation and trust. Waiting on God is never wasted time. Even when answers seem delayed, as in Daniel's story where spiritual resistance held up God's response, the psalm assures us that God hears immediately and is always at work. Faith means trusting His timing, persisting in hope, and continuing to declare His promises even when we can't see the outcome.
The psalm concludes with an exhortation: "Israel, put your hope in the Lord, for with the Lord is unfailing love and with Him is full redemption." (Psalm 130:7) This is not just advice for ancient Israel, but for all who know the struggle of waiting and the sting of loss. God's ability to restore is limitless. Throughout scripture, He has proven Himself faithful—restoring Job's fortunes, lifting the psalmist from the pit, and reconciling lost souls through Christ. God's restoration is not partial or conditional; it is abundant and complete.

Many people, though, hesitate to receive this restoration because they doubt God's promises or try to fill the emptiness with careers, relationships, or material success. Psalm 130 confronts this, reminding us that God alone can truly satisfy. "Seek first the kingdom of God and His righteousness, and all these things shall be added to you" (Matthew 6:33). Make God your highest priority and your ultimate source. When we pursue Him above all else, everything else falls into place.

To pursue God is to recognize that He is not just a helper in times of trouble—He is the essence of life itself. Like a deer thirsting for streams of water (Psalm 42:1), our souls are designed to long for Him. When we seek God first, we experience divine guidance, peace, and the kind of restoration the world cannot offer. No sin, failure, or loss is beyond His power to redeem. The final encouragement of Psalm 130 is clear: Stand on God's word, trust His promises, and watch as He restores what seemed lost. Don't trade your relationship with Him for temporary gains. No matter how deep the pit or how long you've waited, God is near. His faithfulness does not depend on circumstances; it is part of His unchanging nature. If He restored Job, He can restore you. If He lifted the psalmist, He can lift you too.

This psalm is a lifeline for anyone struggling with a guilty conscience or unconfessed sin. Cry out to God for mercy—He forgives quickly and abounds in steadfast love. His faithfulness is not dependent on our circumstances; it is part of His unchanging nature. No situation is beyond His power. Stand on His word, trust His promises, and watch as He restores what seemed lost. If you are in despair, remember: God hears. If you feel unworthy, remember: God forgives and forgets. If you have lost hope, remember: God restores. Above all, pursue Him with all your heart. As you do, you'll find that everything else falls into place.

Psalm 130 is more than a poem—it's a testimony. No matter how deep the pit, how far you've fallen, or how long you've waited, God hears, God forgives, and God restores. His faithfulness is unshakable, and His promises are sure. Seek Him, trust Him, and walk in the fullness of His grace.

Above all, never stop pursuing God. He is indispensable—the only source of true satisfaction, security, and hope. When you seek Him first, all else aligns. Trust Him, seek Him, and experience the fullness of His grace. God hears, God forgives, and God restores.

Chapter 13

Psalm 131: Childlike Trust In The Lord.

1 Lord, my heart is not proud, nor my eyes arrogant;
Nor do I [a]involve myself in great matters,
Or in things too [b]difficult for me.
2 I have certainly soothed and quieted my soul;
Like a weaned child resting [c]against his mother,
My soul [d]within me is like a weaned child.
3 Israel, wait for the Lord
From this time on and forever.

Psalm 131 stands out as a brief yet profound piece of Scripture, offering a radically different vision of strength and contentment. In a world obsessed with ambition, power, and self-promotion, this psalm urges us instead toward humility, quiet confidence and deep trust in God, and the peace that comes from accepting His sovereign wisdom. In just three verses, the psalm offers a countercultural vision of strength—not in self-promotion or ambition, but in contentment and surrender to God's sovereign plan. Whether attributed directly to King David or simply inspired by his experiences, the psalm's message is clear: real strength is found not in assertiveness or relentless striving, but in humble faith and surrendered confidence.

The psalm opens with the title "A song of ascents," suggesting it was sung by pilgrims on their journey to Jerusalem—a journey both literal and spiritual, marked by a conscious laying aside of pride. David's life provides a fitting backdrop for this attitude. Whether being unjustly pursued by Saul or mocked by his own wife Michal for his uninhibited worship, David consistently chose to trust God's timing rather than force his own way. He exemplifies the principle echoed in the New Testament: "God opposes the proud but gives grace to the humble" (James 4:6; 1 Peter 5:5).

Psalm 131 unfolds in three parts, each revealing a step in the art of humility. First, David declares, "O Lord, my heart is not lifted up; my eyes are not raised too high; I do not occupy myself with things too great and too marvelous for me." Here, humility begins with rejecting pride and refusing to be consumed by ambitions too lofty or matters beyond our understanding. True humility, as seen in David, doesn't mean low self-esteem or denying one's abilities. Rather, it's about seeing ourselves rightly before God—acknowledging that every strength and achievement is a gift from Him, not the fruit of our own striving.

The second verse shifts the focus inward: "But I have calmed and quieted my soul, like a weaned child with its mother." This image is rich with meaning. A weaned child no longer cries out in restless need, but rests content in the presence of its mother, trusting provision will come in due time. David's soul, like that child, has learned the hard discipline of stillness before God. In a culture that champions constant achievement and control, learning to quiet our inner restlessness is a challenge. But it is precisely this quiet contentment that marks the truly humble heart. It's not passivity, but an active choice to surrender our agendas and anxieties, and to find peace in God's timing and sufficiency.

The third and final verse turns from personal testimony to communal invitation: "O Israel, hope in the Lord from this time forth and forevermore." David's experience of humble trust becomes a call to the entire community. Humility is not a solitary virtue; it's meant to be lived out in fellowship, encouraging others to place their confidence in God's faithfulness. In a world fraught with anxiety, comparison, and relentless competition, this call could not be more timely. Psalm 131 reminds us that peace and strength are not found in self-advancement, but in yielding to God's plan.

Charles Spurgeon once remarked, "This is one of the shortest psalms to read, but one of the longest to learn." It is deceptively simple yet deeply challenging. The psalm's wisdom is not just theoretical—it offers practical steps for living out humility:

- First, renounce pride by regularly examining your heart. Humility doesn't mean thinking less of yourself, but thinking of yourself accurately before God. Ask: Are you seeking recognition or the approval of others, or are you content to serve quietly, trusting God with your reputation?

- Second, cultivate childlike trust. Like a weaned child, practice resting in God's presence through daily prayer, reflection, and worship. Let go of the need to control outcomes or force opportunities. Learn to be content with what God provides, even when it doesn't align with your immediate desires.

- Third, yield your ambitions to God. Ambition itself isn't wrong, but when it becomes self-centered, it leads to pride. Lay your plans before God and trust Him to open doors in His time rather than pushing ahead to make things happen on your own terms.

At its heart, Psalm 131 reveals that humility is not weakness or insecurity, but the boldest kind of confidence—the kind rooted in God's character and promises, not in our own strength. As we shift our hope from what we can accomplish to what God has promised, we discover a peace that endures.

In a society obsessed with achievement that rewards striving and self-promotion, this psalm calls us to a different way. Its quiet wisdom teaches us that the fullness of life is not found in grasping for more, but in resting in God's sovereign care. Humility frees us from the tyranny of comparison and competition. It gives us the strength to lay aside selfish ambition, embrace the quiet confidence that comes from trusting God and to walk in the beauty of that confidence.

Psalm 131 reminds us that lasting peace and strength are found only in trusting God. May we learn from David's example: to reject pride, quiet our souls, and hope steadfastly in the Lord. True humility is an act of daily surrender—choosing to trust God's timing, to serve without seeking recognition, and to rest in His faithful love. In so doing, we discover that the greatest strength comes not from self-assertion, but from humble dependence on God. Psalm 131 is not a call to passivity or lack of effort, but to a life of surrendered ambition and confident faith offering us this challenging but life-giving path: to walk humbly, to live in peace, and to trust in the Lord forevermore.

In learning to live out Psalm 131, we discover the beauty and strength of a soul at rest in God's sovereign plan—a quiet, weaned soul, untouched by the anxiety of self-advancement. May we all learn the art of humble confidence, finding our peace and purpose in God alone.

Chapter 14

Psalm 132: Prayer For The Lord's Blessing Upon The Sanctuary.

1 Remember, Lord, in David's behalf,
All his affliction;
2 How he swore to the Lord
And vowed to the Mighty One of Jacob,
3 "I certainly will not [a]enter my house,
Nor [b]lie on my bed;
4 I will not give sleep to my eyes
Or slumber to my eyelids,
5 Until I find a place for the Lord,
[c]A dwelling place for the Mighty One of Jacob."
6 Behold, we heard about it in Ephrathah,
We found it in the field of [d]Jaar.
7 Let's go into His [e]dwelling place;
Let's worship at His footstool.
8 Arise, Lord, to Your resting place,
You and the ark of Your strength.
9 May Your priests be clothed with righteousness,
And may Your godly ones sing for joy.
10 For the sake of Your servant David,
Do not turn away the face of Your anointed.
11 The Lord has sworn to David
A truth from which He will not turn back:
"I will set upon your throne one from the fruit of your body.
12 If your sons will keep My covenant
And My testimony which I will teach them,

Their sons also will sit upon your throne forever."
13 For the Lord has chosen Zion;
He has desired it as His dwelling place.
14 "This is My resting place forever;
Here I will dwell, for I have desired it.
15 I will abundantly bless her food;
I will satisfy her needy with bread.
16 I will also clothe her priests with salvation,
And her godly ones will sing aloud for joy.
17 I will make the horn of David spring forth there;
I have prepared a lamp for My anointed.
18 I will clothe his enemies with shame,
But upon himself his crown will gleam."

Psalm 132, a psalm that stands apart in both length and content from the other Songs of Ascents. Unlike the shorter, more lyrical and meditative psalms, Psalm 132 unfolds as an epic poem with a distinct narrative quality, recounting the story of David's arrival in Jerusalem with the Ark of the Covenant, David's fervent desire to build a dwelling place for God and the divine promise given to him through the prophet Nathan, as chronicled in 2 Samuel 7. This psalm weaves together Israel's history, David's passion for God, God's covenantal promises, and the profound theme of Zion as God's chosen dwelling.

Psalm 132's significance lies not only in its recounting of historic events but also in its theological depth. Zion is featured prominently—referred to as the dwelling place of God in multiple verses (5, 7, 8, 13)—underscoring the idea that God's presence resides among His people and that His blessings flow from this holy place. The psalm also repeatedly references David, highlighting both his hardships and his pivotal role as the Lord's anointed, and focusing on God's promises to his lineage- a promise that ripples through history, faith, and the very heart of Christian hope.

To fully appreciate Psalm 132, reading 2 Samuel 7 is invaluable. David's fervent desire to build a house for the Lord—evident in his efforts to bring the Ark of the Covenant to Jerusalem and establish a permanent temple—

sets the stage for God's remarkable promise: that one of David's descendants would perpetually occupy Israel's throne. Verses 6–10 of the psalm celebrate the joyous arrival of the Ark in Jerusalem, capturing the collective longing to worship at God's dwelling and reflecting both David's vision and the people's aspirations. The psalm goes on to recount God's covenant with David, promising enduring kingship to his descendants, provided they remain faithful to God's commands.

But Psalm 132 is not merely a celebration of the past; it is also a plea for God to honor His commitments, especially in times of uncertainty, and a source of hope for future blessings. For Christians, the psalm points ahead to Jesus Christ, who fulfills God's promise to David by rising from the dead and reigning eternally.

This understanding leads us to a crucial lesson: God's promises, while certain, are not passively received. There is a way to accelerate their fulfillment. Many believers wait for God's blessings, unaware that God often moves at the level of our commitment and devotion. David's life is a striking example of this principle. When he received a word from God, he didn't sit back—he acted, prayed, and pursued God's purposes with passion. Similarly, Daniel, upon discovering the prophecy that Israel's captivity would last seventy years, responded with urgent prayer and fasting, not complacency (Daniel 9:2-3). Anna the prophetess, likewise, prayed faithfully for the fulfillment of the prophecy concerning Jesus (Luke 2:36-38).

This is the heart of Psalm 132's commentary: David's uncompromising dedication to God unlocked unprecedented favor and an eternal covenant. His sacrifices and persistent pursuit of God's agenda were not acts of pride, but demonstrations of covenantal faith. As Isaiah 62:6-7 puts it, God invites His people to remind Him of His promises and to give Him no rest until His word is fulfilled. Reminding God of His promises is not unbelief; it is a bold act of faith.

Yet, the fulfillment of God's promises requires obedience. God's oath to David—"I will place on your throne the offspring of your loins... if your sons walk in My covenant..." (Psalm 132:11-12)—makes it clear that we have a role to play. David's faithfulness resulted not just in personal blessing but in generational blessing, ultimately fulfilled in Jesus Christ (Luke 1:32-33).

This brings us to a common misinterpretation of Matthew 6:33: "But seek first the kingdom of God and His righteousness, and all these things shall be added to you." Many read this as a call to focus only on spiritual pursuits, neglecting earthly responsibilities. This misunderstanding has, at times, led believers into poverty and reduced their impact on society. Yet, Matthew 6:33 does not call us to abandon our earthly ambitions, but to integrate them with a primary focus on God's kingdom. "Seek first" means that as we engage in work, relationships, and personal growth, our first priority should be aligning these endeavors with God's principles.

David exemplifies this harmonious balance. Though a king with countless responsibilities, he made the building of a temple for God his foremost pursuit. Psalm 132:3-5 recounts his vow not to rest until he found a dwelling place for the Lord. His life teaches us that seeking God's kingdom first is not about neglecting other goals, but about infusing every part of life—business, relationships, talents—with kingdom values and divine purpose.

This balanced approach does not mean setting aside personal aspirations or material needs. Rather, it encourages excellence in all areas, guided by God's principles, with the assurance that God will meet our needs. When our work, finances, and dreams are aligned with God's will, we mirror David's example and position ourselves for God's promises and blessing.

Furthermore, David's zeal for God's work was about more than building a physical temple; it was about bringing God's presence closer to His people. The Ark of the Covenant symbolized God's indwelling presence among Israel. In Psalm 132:6-9, the psalmist remembers the journey of the Ark and calls the people to worship at God's footstool. David's longing was not for occasional encounters with God, but for a permanent, abiding relationship— just as Jesus later urges His followers to "abide in Me, and I in you" (John 15:4).

Today, the challenge is to make God's presence central in every aspect of our lives. It's not enough to commune with God only in church on Sundays; we must pursue Him daily, letting His presence shape our decisions, relationships, and pursuits. The more we seek God, the more His presence and power are manifest in our lives.

David's life also reminds us that pleasing God first does not lead to lack, but to prosperity, effectiveness, and fulfillment. Proverbs 11:25 says, "A generous soul will be made rich, and he who waters will also be watered himself." David "watered the ground" by seeking God's kingdom first, investing his time, money, and energy in God's priorities. As a result, God established David's legacy and secured his descendants.

For many Christians, the problem is not that they do not ask God, but that their desires are self-centered rather than kingdom-centered (James 4:2-3). Psalm 132 is a call to align our goals with God's purposes, to passionately pursue what brings God glory, and to trust that He will take care of our needs.

Psalm 132 challenges believers to pursue God's kingdom with the same passion as David. This means:

- Making God's will the filter for every decision and ambition.

- Welcoming God's presence into every area of life, not just spiritual "corners."

- Praying persistently for God's promises to be fulfilled, both personally and corporately.

- Investing time, resources, and energy into what brings God glory and advances His purposes on earth.

In closing, the true lesson of Psalm 132—and the life of David—is that spiritual commitment is not at odds with earthly achievement. One can seek God's kingdom and have earthly effectiveness. David's example shows that making God's kingdom our highest priority brings both spiritual and material blessing. Spiritual commitment and worldly achievement are not at odds but are deeply compatible when God's priorities come first. Jesus' words in Matthew 6:33 —"seek first the kingdom", are not a call to neglect life's responsibilities or asceticism, but to place God first in everything within our holistic and integrated living. When we do this ,put God first as David did, God's promises that "all these things shall be added" become reality in our lives with purpose, provision and fulfillment.

Psalm 132 is not just a song of ancient Israel; it is a roadmap for every believer who longs for a life of meaning, blessing, and impact. David's example calls us to passionate devotion, practical obedience, and persistent faith. A life devoted to God's purposes is one that thrives, impacts the world, and secures blessings that endure beyond time. When we put God's kingdom first— truly first—everything else begins to fall into place. Psalm 132 calls us to this kind of life—a life where seeking God first is the foundation for everything else, and where God's presence and promises are established in our lives and our greatest treasure.

Chapter 15

Psalm 133: The Excellence of Brotherly Unity.

1 Behold, how good and how pleasant it is
For brothers to live together in unity!
2 It is like the precious oil on the head,
Running down upon the beard,
As on Aaron's beard,
The oil which ran down upon the edge of his robes.
3 It is like the dew of Hermon
Coming down upon the mountains of Zion;
For the Lord commanded the blessing there—life forever.

When there is real unity in the church, the anointing flows freely, miracles abound, and the gospel advances with power. The psalm uses images of hospitality and nature to illustrate God's welcoming presence and links unity to joy and peace, as celebrated in songs sung by pilgrims journeying to Jerusalem. Unity is crucial for building a peaceful Christian community and for countering the negative impacts of division. The Apostle Paul underscored the importance of unity, viewing it as a divine command, and Ephesians advocates for breaking down barriers and nurturing unity, mirroring Jesus' teachings.

Psalm 133 stands as a powerful meditation on the significance, beauty and necessity of unity among believers. It opens with a declaration: "Behold, how good and how pleasant it is for brethren to dwell together in unity!" Unlike many things in life that are good but not pleasant, or pleasant but not good, unity is both. It is pleasing to God and deeply beneficial for His people. The psalm uses vivid imagery—the precious anointing oil on Aaron's head and the refreshing dew of Hermon falling on Mount Zion—to show how unity is not just good in theory, but a channel of God's very blessing, culminating in the promise of eternal life. Unity is deeply associated with God's blessings—especially the blessing of eternal life.

Unity is more than just an ideal; it is the fragrance of heaven, the oil that flows from the throne of grace, anointing the body of Christ and making the church a force that cannot be ignored and must be reckoned with. When unity is real and present in the church , God's anointing flows freely, miracles abound, and the gospel advances with power. The psalm uses images of hospitality and nature to illustrate God's welcoming presence and links unity to joy and peace, as celebrated in songs sung by pilgrims journeying to Jerusalem. Unity is crucial for building a peaceful Christian community and for countering the negative impacts of division. The Apostle Paul underscored the importance of unity, viewing it as a divine command, and Ephesians advocates for breaking down barriers and nurturing unity, mirroring Jesus' teachings.

This unity the psalmist speaks of in pslams 133 mirrors the oneness of the Godhead—Father, Son, and Spirit—and is the climate in which God's presence dwells. Acts 2:1-4 shows the early church gathered in one accord at Pentecost; it was this very unity that provided the backdrop for the outpouring of the Holy Spirit and the explosive growth of the early church. Unfortunately, the enemy has always understood the spiritual power that unity unlocks. From the beginning, Satan's strategy has been to sow division—whether in marriages, families, or the wider church. As Jesus warned in Mark 3:25, "If a house is divided against itself, that house cannot stand." Division is the devil's most effective tool because he knows a fractured church is spiritually impotent. He targets relationships, sows discord, and exploits differences, especially through denominationalism.

Denominationalism itself is not inherently evil—God delights in diversity and variety. He created every individual with unique gifts, cultures, and talents so that the body of Christ could be rich and multifaceted. The early church reflected this diversity, and the Songs of Ascents (Psalms 120–134) were sung by pilgrims from every tribe as they journeyed to Jerusalem, united by faith and purpose. Even as denominations emerged to organize theology and church government, the enemy twisted this diversity into rivalry and alienation, fueling wars and conflicts that hindered the advance of the gospel. Yet God's vision is not erased by our differences. Instead, our diversity should become a source of mutual enrichment, not division. The church is called to rise above labels and tradition, focusing on what unites us: Jesus Christ, the gospel, and the call to love one another. As Ephesians 4:3 urges, we are to "strive to maintain the unity of the Spirit in the bond of peace." Paul repeatedly called believers to live peaceably and to be "perfectly joined together in the same mind and in the same judgment" (1 Corinthians 1:10), knowing that unity is the secret to the church's vitality and testimony to the world.

Psalm 133's metaphors drive this point home. The anointing oil poured on Aaron's head did not stop at the head but flowed down, consecrating his whole body for service. In the same way, Christ is the head of the church, and unity allows His anointing and power to flow to every member. Any part disconnected from the body misses out on this blessing. The dew of Hermon is a symbol of divine enablement—just as dew sustains life in a dry land, unity brings spiritual renewal and vitality to the church. This "dew" is not something humans can manufacture; it is a supernatural gift, the work of the Holy Spirit.

When believers set aside competition, pride, and self-interest—choosing instead forgiveness, humility, and love—they create a climate where God's blessing can rest. The early church modeled this: they devoted themselves to teaching, fellowship, breaking of bread, and prayer. Their unity was practical, sacrificial, and powerful, resulting in daily growth and miracles (Acts 2:42-47). Unity, then, is not merely an option but a divine mandate—Jesus prayed for it before going to the cross (John 17:21-23), knowing it would be the church's greatest witness to the world.

Yet unity does not mean uniformity. God's purpose is not to erase our differences but to bring us together in a shared mission. Denominations, when rightly understood, can celebrate God's creativity, provided they do not become barriers to fellowship. As Romans 12:18 instructs, "If it is possible, as far as it depends on you, live at peace with everyone." Gossip, quarreling, and self-seeking are to be replaced with humility, forgiveness, and sincere love.

Much is at stake. A divided church cannot advance God's kingdom, but when believers walk in harmony, God commands His blessing—life forevermore. The church's unity is not just a matter of fellowship but of spiritual authority and divine manifestation. As the commentary on Psalm 133 reminds us, unity revives and refreshes, while discord dries up spiritual life. The devil will continue to attack unity, but believers are called to resist—standing together, loving each other in humility, and focusing on Christ above all.

Let us therefore pursue the unity celebrated in Psalm 133. Let us experience the abundance of life, the flow of God's anointing, and the expansion of His kingdom as we walk together in love. Unity is not just a dream but God's mandate and the secret to living in the fullness of His blessing.

Chapter 16

Psalm 134: Greetings Of Night Watchers.

1 Behold, bless the Lord, all you servants of the Lord,
Who [a]serve by night in the house of the Lord!
2 Lift up your hands to the sanctuary
And bless the Lord.
3 May the Lord bless you from Zion,
He who made heaven and earth.

We have come to the end of our journey through the Songs of Ascents. After exploring these psalms—sixteen studies deep—it's striking to look back over the path we've traveled. From the opening cry of exile and longing in Psalm 120 to this last, brief celebration in Psalm 134, we've witnessed a pilgrim's journey: from scattered hardship to the joy of God's presence. This final psalm is not just a closing note but a triumphant crescendo, calling God's people to a life of worship and blessing. Psalm 134, the shortest of these songs, marks our arrival at the destination.

This psalm is both a conclusion and a new beginning. The journey that started in the wilderness—far from peace, with desperate pleas for help—ends in the sanctuary, in the very presence of God. The pilgrims, weary but hopeful, are welcomed into God's house, united with other believers, and called to a life of praise. Imagine standing in the stillness of the night, hands lifted, heart full of praise, eyes looking up to heaven. The darkness around you fades in the presence of the Almighty. This is the scene Psalm 134 paints: "Come, bless the Lord, all you servants of the Lord, who stand by night in the house of the Lord! Lift up your hands to the holy place and bless the Lord! May the Lord bless you from Zion, he who made heaven and earth."

Psalm 134 isn't just a song to close a chapter; it's a call to take up a lifelong stance of worship. The words, "Bless the Lord," echo throughout, not as a suggestion but as a command—an invitation to praise God at all times, in all circumstances. This phrase isn't just about singing; it's about honoring God, recognizing His majesty, and declaring His goodness, whether we feel it or not.

Imagine the scene: servants of the Lord—priests and Levites—standing in the temple at night. The city sleeps, but their hands are lifted, their hearts full, eyes turned heavenward. In the darkness, they declare, through praise, that God reigns and is worthy. Their worship was not a mere gesture, but a spiritual position—a way to invite God's presence, protection, and blessing. Today, that call stretches beyond the temple walls. All believers are summoned to continuous worship, not as a Sunday ritual, but as a lifestyle that fills both days and nights. True worship is steadfast, persisting through trials, fear, uncertainty, and joy alike.

In ancient times, watchmen guarded the city walls at night, ready to sound the alarm at the first sign of danger. Psalm 134 draws this parallel: every believer is a spiritual watchman, standing guard over their life, family, church, and destiny with praise as their weapon.

When the psalm says, "all you servants of the Lord, who by night stand in the house of the Lord," it's highlighting the importance of watching and worshipping—especially during life's "night seasons," literal and figurative. Praise, then, becomes a spiritual strategy. Just as watchmen keep out invaders, praise keeps out despair, fear, and spiritual attack.

The Bible is loaded with stories of breakthrough that began with worship:

- **Paul and Silas in Prison:** At midnight, bruised and shackled, they sang hymns. God shook the earth, chains broke, and the doors flew open (Acts 16:25-26).

- **Jehoshaphat's Victory:** Facing a hopeless battle, the king sent singers ahead of his army. Their praise confused the enemy and brought victory (2 Chronicles 20:21-22).

- **Walls of Jericho:** The Israelites' shout of praise brought down the city walls (Joshua 6).

Praise is not passive. When we bless the Lord as watchmen, we:

- Secure God's protection (Psalm 91:1-2)
- Shut the gates against spiritual enemies (Isaiah 62:6)
- Draw God's presence into our circumstances (Psalm 22:3)

"Lift up your hands to the holy place and bless the Lord!" (Psalm 134:2). Lifting hands in worship is more than a symbol; it's a spiritual posture—surrender, victory, and openness to receive from God. Throughout Scripture, this act is linked to breakthrough:

Moses' Uplifted Hands: As long as his hands were raised in prayer, Israel prevailed over Amalek (Exodus 17:11-12).

- **David's Thanksgiving:** "Let the lifting up of my hands be as the evening sacrifice" (Psalm 141:2).

- **Jesus Blessing His Disciples:** He raised His hands as He ascended (Luke 24:50-51).

Worship in this way isn't about performance or feeling. It's about faith, aligning ourselves with God's will, and preparing for supernatural encounters. When we worship—especially in the darkness—we're not just giving to God; we're opening ourselves to receive from Him.

Psalm 134 closes with a benediction: "May the Lord bless you from Zion, he who made heaven and earth." Here, the movement shifts from the praise of the people to the blessing of God. It's a divine exchange: as we bless God, He blesses us in return. The Creator who made heaven and earth is not distant; He promises to be with us, to provide, protect, and sustain, wherever our journey takes us.

This blessing isn't confined to the physical temple or a particular city; it goes with the people of God into their everyday lives. As Jesus promised, "I am with you always, to the end of the age" (Matthew 28:20).

Life is a journey of mountaintops and valleys, joy and hardship. Psalm 134 teaches that worship isn't just for the good times. The real test is whether we can bless the Lord in the storm. True worshippers praise God not for what He does, but for who He is.

When Paul and Silas praised God in their suffering, their worship became a spiritual sword—breaking chains and leading to salvation. When Job lost everything, he still said, "Blessed be the name of the Lord" (Job 1:21). Worship shifts our focus from problems to promises, from trials to triumphs. Throughout the Bible, those who worshipped encountered God in profound ways:

- **Isaiah's Vision:** Worship in the temple led to a life-changing revelation (Isaiah 6:1-8).

- **Solomon's Temple:** Worship brought God's glory like a cloud (2 Chronicles 7:1-3).

- **Shepherds at Jesus' Birth:** Worship led them to witness the Messiah's glory (Luke 2:8-14).

Worship is how we move from seeking blessings to seeking the Blesser. Worship is not circumstantial or emotional; it's an act of faith and reverence. As we respond to the call to worship, we open the door for God's presence, power, and transformation.

Worship, then, is not just giving to God—it is also the means by which we receive from Him. When we answer the call to worship, we open ourselves to divine encounters, breakthroughs, and supernatural blessings. Throughout Scripture, those who worshipped—Isaiah in the temple, Solomon at the dedication, the shepherds at Christ's birth—were transformed by God's glory. Worship shifts our focus from problems to promises and positions us to experience God's presence and power.

Psalm 134 teaches us that worship is both our duty and our privilege. It is the key to living as spiritual watchmen, securing protection, drawing God's presence, and shutting the gates against the enemy. Whether in the darkness of night or the brightness of day, in hardship or in joy, our call is to bless the Lord. This is not simply for what He has done, but for who He is—the Lord, maker of heaven and earth.

Psalm 134 leaves us with a challenge and a promise. The challenge: will we answer the call to worship, not as a ritual but as a way of life? Will we stand as spiritual watchmen, blessing the Lord in every season—joy or hardship, day or night?

The promise: when we lift our hands, bless the Lord, and stand in worship, God meets us there. He blesses, protects, and goes with us on the road ahead.

If you seek breakthrough, intimacy with God, and supernatural encounter, the invitation is clear: worship. Raise your hands, lift your voice, and bless the Lord—your encounter with God awaits.

May God bless and keep you, strengthen and encourage you as you continue your journey, and fill your life with His presence and peace.

The psalm closes with a benediction: "May the Lord bless you from Zion, he who made heaven and earth." Here, we see a divine exchange—when we bless the Lord, He blesses us in return. The Creator of heaven and earth, whose presence once dwelled in Zion, now promises to go with us wherever we are. Even as the pilgrims left Jerusalem to return to their daily lives, God's blessing would remain with them. This echoes Jesus' promise: "I am with you always, to the end of the age" (Matthew 28:20).

So as we end this journey through the Songs of Ascents, remember: the path does not end here. We continue as pilgrims, walking through life's challenges and joys, called to praise, to watchfulness, and to faith. If you desire breakthrough, intimacy with God, or supernatural encounters, answer the call to worship. Lift your hands, bless the Lord, and see how He will move in your life. God can and will bless and keep you, strengthen and encourage you, and fill your heart with songs of praise as you continue your journey. Will you raise your hands today and respond: "Bless the Lord, O my soul"? Your encounter with God awaits.

Chapter 17

Closing Thoughts!

The Lord bless you
and keep you;
the Lord make his face shone on you
and be gracious to you;
the Lord turn his face toward you
and give you peace!
Numbers 6: 24-26 NIV

As we bring this journey to a close, I want to express my deep gratitude for walking with me through the Songs of Ascent. Together, we have explored Psalms 120–134—not merely as literary artifacts or theological curiosities, but as living expressions of faith that speak powerfully into our lives today. These psalms were once sung by pilgrims ascending toward Jerusalem, and now they rise again in our hearts as songs of worship, hope, and spiritual renewal.

The central theme of these fifteen psalms is ascent—both literal and spiritual. The Israelites sang them on their way to the temple, but their words transcend geography. They chart a path from distress to deliverance, from isolation to unity, from doubt to trust, and ultimately from earth to heaven. Each psalm serves as a step on a sacred staircase, guiding us closer to God's presence. Whether it was Psalm 121's assurance of divine protection, Psalm 127's reminder of God's sovereignty over human labor, or Psalm 133's call to godly unity, every song offers a unique yet unified vision of what it means to live under the Lord's watchful care.

One of the lingering questions many readers ask is why these psalms are grouped together at all. While scholars debate the exact origins and function of the collection, one thing remains clear: the Songs of Ascent were intended for communal use. They were not written for solitary reflection alone, but for corporate worship, shared experience, and mutual encouragement. In a day when individualism often overshadows community, these psalms remind us that our faith is meant to be lived out among others—worshipping together, praying together, and growing together in Christ.

Another important insight is how deeply practical these psalms are. They don't offer abstract theology—they give us language for real life. They teach us how to cry out in pain (Psalm 120), how to trust in times of uncertainty (Psalm 121), how to long for God's house (Psalm 122), how to seek peace (Psalm 125), how to bless others (Psalm 128), and how to rejoice in God's mercy (Psalm 130). They model a spirituality that is grounded, honest, and full of grace.

I also want to address a question that may still linger in your mind: How do these psalms connect to Jesus? Though written centuries before His coming, the Songs of Ascent point forward to the ultimate Pilgrim—our Lord and Savior—who walked the roads of Galilee and Judea, who made His final ascent to Jerusalem to suffer, die, and rise again for our salvation. In Him, the pilgrimage reaches its fulfillment. He is both the destination and the guide. And in reading these psalms through the lens of the gospel, we find deeper meaning and greater joy.

My prayer is that this book has not only informed your mind but transformed your heart. More than knowledge, I pray you've gained a renewed hunger for God's Word, a deeper reverence for His presence, and a stronger desire to walk closely with Him each day. Let this not be the end of your journey, but the beginning of a lifelong pursuit of holiness, unity, and worship.

To continue growing in your relationship with Christ, I encourage you to keep studying Scripture—not just the Psalms, but all of God's Word. Read widely. Reflect deeply. Pray continually. Share what you've learned with others. Consider starting a small group study on the Songs of Ascent in your church, or preaching a sermon series that leads your congregation upward in faith. The beauty of these psalms is that they are meant to be lived and shared, not simply read and remembered..

About the Author

Dr. John R. Sconiers, II, DMin, is a senior pastor, preacher, mentor, board certified chaplain and evangelism coordinator. Dr. Sconiers' education includes DMin in evangelism and church planting, DIT in Security, MAPM (MDIV Equivalent), MIS Security, BSIT as well as postgraduate work in counseling and theology. He also holds several certifications and has hosted numerous training sessions in the area of evangelism, small groups, and other topics. Dr. Sconiers has lived and preached in various parts of the world and has a passion for seeing lives transformed by the power of the Holy Spirit and seeks to point others to the good news of Jesus Christ. Dr. Sconiers currently serves as a senior pastor in the North Georgia area. He is married to one wife, Nicole, and they share five amazing children.

You can connect with Dr. John R Sconiers II via:

Instagram: @johnsconiers
Twitter: @johnsconiers
YouTube: @JohnSconiers
Email: John@johnsconiersministries.com
Website: https://www.johnsconiersministries.com

www.ingramcontent.com/pod-product-compliance
Lightning Source LLC
Chambersburg PA
CBHW071341130626
46556CB00004B/1979